I took up Carole's challenge and gave God a year, and it has been the best year of my life. I feel younger, thinner, wiser, stronger and more motivated, energized and in tune with God and His adventure for my life. If every person would give God a year, we would all learn how to give Him our minutes, hours and days in a way that would not only benefit us personally but also benefit the world. It is a complete win-win to give God a year!

Pam Farrel
International speaker and author,
Men Are Like Waffles, Women Are Like Spaghetti

Carole Lewis is an encourager and a motivator! *Give God a Year* outlines practical steps that will permanently change your life for the better. Last January, I accepted her challenge to combine physical exercise, portion and calorie control at mealtimes and spiritual disciplines in my daily routine. Now, 25 pounds lighter, I know I can finish strong! Thank you, Carole, for revealing the secrets to personal and spiritual wellbeing.

Carol Kent
Speaker and author, *Becoming a Woman of Influence*

I dare you to follow Carole Lewis's challenge to Give God a Year and see how He changes you from the inside out! I'm about three-fourths of the way through my "year" and have learned so much from Carole's testimony of laying out our part and God's part—and then diligently learning to trust and obey His principles. If you've tried everything else but to no avail, why not try relinquishment? This book will show you how real people can make substantial changes even in the midst of life's interruptions and challenges. Go for it and see what God will accomplish *in* you and *through* you in the next 12 months!

Lucinda Secrest McDowell
Author, *Spa for the Soul* and *God's Purpose for You*

On the surface, a year can seem like a very long time. But one year = 365 days = 8,760 hours = 525,600 minutes that pass by very quickly. Carole's challenge to Give God a Year is one I intend to take. I am certain that, with the help of this book, when those 525,600 minutes have passed I will be more of the woman Christ has called me to be. How about you? Don't let the minutes slip away . . . Give God a Year!

Kendra Smiley
Author and conference speaker
www.KendraSmiley.com

GIVE GOD A YEAR, CHANGE YOUR LIFE FOREVER!

Carole Lewis

Regal

From Gospel Light
Ventura, California, U.S.A.

Published by Regal
From Gospel Light
Ventura, California, U.S.A.
www.regalbooks.com
Printed in the U.S.A.

Library of Congress Cataloging-in-Publication Data
Lewis, Carole, 1942-
Give God a year, change your life forever / Carole Lewis.
p. cm.
ISBN 978-0-8307-5132-7 (hard cover)
1. Spirituality—Christianity. I. Title.
BV4501.3.L496 2009
248.4—dc22
2009034664

1 2 3 4 5 6 7 8 9 10 / 15 14 13 12 11 10 09

Rights for publishing this book outside the U.S.A. or in non-English
languages are administered by Gospel Light Worldwide, an international
not-for-profit ministry. For additional information, please visit www.glww.org,
email info@glww.org, or write to Gospel Light Worldwide,
1957 Eastman Avenue, Ventura, CA 93003, U.S.A.

CONTENTS

ACKNOWLEDGMENTS

I want to thank all the men and women in our First Place 4 Health family for your prayers and support this past year. You stood with us after Hurricane Ike and your love and concern have truly been the wind beneath our wings. I've sent chapters of this book to some of you for your comments, and your feedback has been more valuable than you will ever know.

Thank you to Pat Lewis for all your hard work to make this book the best it can be. Your help is so valuable in a project such as this and your love and support are a true gift from God.

Thank you to Regal Books for believing in me and encouraging me to press on this past year. You are family to me.

INTRODUCTION

Where would you like to be a year from today?

What would you like to see yourself doing? Do you want a better job? Where would you like to be living? Does your marriage need healing? Does your family need to come back to God? Do you want to have a baby? Do you want to be married? Do you want to have a best friend? Would you like to lose a lot of weight? Do you desire better health? Does your life need balance? Do you want to get out of debt? Do you need a better car? Would you like to know God better?

Dig down deep in the recesses of your heart, soul, mind and body and spend some time contemplating these questions. You might know the answers immediately or you might need to pray and ask God to show them to you. It really doesn't matter how long it takes to come to the answers, but after you have determined the greatest needs in your own life, take time to write them down. Your list may be really long, but once you've finished making the list, go back and pick your top five greatest needs or desires that you would like to see fulfilled in the next year.

1. _____

2. _____

3. _____

4. _____

5. _____

Think about what your life would look like a year from today if these five things could change in the right direction. Our God has the power to radically change people, circumstances and situations. He owns the cattle on a thousand hills, so money and other resources are not a problem for Him. He knows us better than we know ourselves and wants to help us change for the better. God still performs miracles today, so even if the five things you listed above seem hopeless to you, they are not a problem to God.

Now here's the question I want to ask you: Are you willing to give God the next year of your life? I'm talking about 7 days a week, 52 weeks in a row, for a total of 12 whole months, one right after the other.

Change that will last does not happen quickly, but a year will pass quickly, whether you accept the challenge or not. A year from now you can be in exactly the same spot you are today or your life can be radically different. The choice is yours. You have the power to change direction, but do you want to?

If you accept the challenge, I promise that you will never be sorry and you will be forever grateful that you picked up this book.

But what is the challenge? Keep reading . . .

GIVE GOD A YEAR, CHANGE YOUR LIFE FOREVER!

1

For the eyes of the LORD range throughout the earth to
strengthen those whose hearts are fully committed to him.

2 CHRONICLES 16:9

After spending a couple of years rewriting the First Place program, the new materials were released in July 2008 under a new name, First Place 4 Health. When the writing was finally completed, followed by weeks of editing, and when the new program was shipped, we were able to take a look at the fruit of all our hard work. The new program consists of 12-week sessions, but we all knew that it is impossible to have a complete lifestyle change in 12 weeks. For this reason, we asked each of the participants to "give us a year" to see what God could do.

July was a frenzy of preparation for our annual First Place 4 Health Leadership Summit held each year in Houston. We had a record number of leaders from 32 states and from Canada who were anxious to see the new program and learn how to lead it. A glorious time was had by all, culminating with an afternoon and evening at our home on Galveston bay. We were still basking in the afterglow of the Leadership Summit when August was upon us.

Our publisher graciously hired a publicity agency to promote the new program so August was full of newspaper and radio interviews about First Place 4 Health. Each month we write articles for our First Place 4 Health e-Newsletter and our deadline is the fifteenth of the month. Well, the fifteenth came and went and everyone but me had written and turned in their articles. When I left work on Friday, August 22, I promised that my article would be ready on Monday.

I thought about the article all day Saturday but still didn't find time to write it, but Sunday at 3:15 A.M., my eyes popped open. I was instantly awake. I got up and spent some time reading my Bible and praying, and then sat down at my computer to write the article below:

Dear Friends,

This is Sunday morning and I got up very early to write this article, which, by the way, is now nine days late! As I sat having my quiet time, I was reading my *One Year Bible*. Today's reading was in Job, chapters 12–15. I always ask the Lord, "What do You have for me in today's reading?" I chuckled as I thought about writing an encouraging, motivating article for you on the book of Job!

Yesterday was Saturday and we spent a quiet day at home. Since the First Place 4 Health Leadership Summit at the end of July, we have had company almost continuously. I so enjoyed staying in my robe till noon just puttering around the house doing a few small chores. One of those chores was changing the light bulbs in the ceiling fan in the room where I write. There was also another ceiling light in the room that had burned out, so I thought it was a perfect day to change these bulbs. When I took off the covers, I discovered that all of the bulbs needed to be 60-watt and I didn't have one in the house. I shared my dilemma with Johnny and he suggested that I use some new fluorescent bulbs we had bought, so I set about to do just that. The new bulbs are larger than traditional bulbs, but I was able to get the globe back on the ceiling fan with just a little gap. It felt tight even though it was not flush with the base.

As I walked into the room where my computer sat, finally ready to write the article at 4:15 A.M. this morning, I reached for the string to turn on the light under the ceiling fan. As the light came on, the globe fell off and exploded as it hit the floor. Fifteen minutes later, after sweeping up a gazillion pieces of glass, I sat down to write this article. I was reminded of what I had read earlier in the book of Job, but then the Lord sweetly reminded me that my reading in the New Testament was from 1 Corinthians and included one of my favorite memory verses: "Therefore, my dear brothers (and sisters), stand firm. Let nothing move you. Always give yourselves fully to the work of the Lord, because you know that your labor in the Lord is not in vain" (1 Corinthians 15:58).

September is here—a new school year, a new fall season of First Place 4 Health with an entirely new program. I'm sure your life is much like mine has been this morning: a lot going on and challenges all along the way. I want to issue a challenge to each of you reading this article to give God a year to make you into the kind of man or woman who can "stand firm and let nothing move you." God has a wonderful plan for your life and for mine, but He needs our cooperation to accomplish all He has planned for us.

Let me close with a story that I believe conveys what is in my heart this morning. In October 2007, I met a woman whose name is Jan Norris. Jan went to the Internet and Googled "spa." Expensive spa weeks came up, so she Googled "Christian spa," and our First Place 4 Health Spa Week came up. Jan came to Round Top, Texas, in October 2007 without a clue about what she could expect. We gave each participant a pedometer the first day and challenged them to set a goal to walk 10,000 steps a day at least one day before the week was over.

The first morning, I met all the people who were not up to aerobics in the barn to go out for a walk. Jan was in the group and I thought to myself, "I bet she won't be able to walk five minutes." But as we were walking, Jan said to me, "You are going to see a lot less of me next year." Before the week was out, Jan walked the 10,000 steps in one day, which, by the way, is about 5 miles. Jan went home from Spa Week and drove an hour each week to attend a First Place 4 Health class. In January 2008, she started leading a group in her church.

Jan gave her testimony at our Leadership Summit in July and has now lost 100 pounds! When the leaders came to our home on Saturday afternoon, I wanted to cry as I saw Jan get into a kayak and paddle all over the bay and then later ride the Triple Dare, a water toy pulled behind the boat.

Do you realize that in one year you could lose 100 pounds? You could become a person who exercises regularly? You could find balance spiritually by having a quiet time every day? You could memorize 52 Bible verses by memorizing one verse each week? A year seems like such a long time, but it will be over before we blink an eye.

If today you decide to give God a year by giving Christ first place every day, I promise you won't be sorry!

After I finished writing the article, I sat in front of my computer, preparing to email the article to the office so that it would be there first thing Monday morning. As I was sitting there, I heard the still, small voice of the Holy Spirit speak to me as He has so many times before. I love it when He speaks to me, but He speaks so softly, and is so gentle and kind, that many times I am too busy to hear His voice. This particular morning I heard Him say to me, "Would you give Me a year and see what I can do in your own life?"

Well, I needed some time to consider this question, so I thought and prayed about it all day Sunday. By Sunday night I had accepted the challenge, knowing full well that God had invited me to go on a journey with Him that, though it wouldn't be easy, would undoubtedly be exciting.

I began early Monday morning, August 25, 2008, on my commitment to give God the next year of my life. I can truthfully say that the first four days of that week were the best four days that I had experienced in a long time. What had I done differently that week than I'd been doing before? Well, to put it mildly, *everything*.

In the frenzy of writing and getting ready for the Leadership Summit I had relapsed into some bad habits. We have a saying: When the going gets tough . . . First Place 4 Health people *eat*. Not only had I been overeating, but I had neglected my quiet time so much that I had started bringing in the newspaper at 4:00 A.M. and reading it instead of spending time with God. I was in such a sad state that a week before the Leadership Summit, I still didn't know what I was going to say to the group of leaders.

God took pity on me and graciously gave my talk to Vicki Heath. Vicki was obedient and wrote down what she had heard from God, but she knew the words weren't for her to share. She called our office and shared the message with my assistant, Pat. After hearing what Vicki had to say, Pat told her that I still didn't know what I was going to talk about and asked Vicki to call me. I will never forget that conversation. Vicki said that it was so strange the way the message had come so fast—she had to grab the nearest tablet and write it down. Vicki's husband, Rob, was in Iraq at the time, and when they talked by phone, Vicki shared what had happened and Rob said, "Sounds like a presidential message to me."

Now, I've given a lot of messages, and many times they are late in coming, but I have never—no, never—given a message that was transmitted to me through someone else's body! This was a first, but I was so desperate that I thanked Vicki and asked her to email her notes. I gave the message, which was on love, at the Leadership Summit and no one was the wiser . . . until now!

I can see clearly today that God was at work to show me just how great, good, powerful and loving He really is. He knew all along about the invitation He was about to give me and that I would accept the challenge.

After only four days of taking the challenge, the Lord woke me very early to give me the plan for the year. It amounted to only two words, but those two words have the power to change you and me forever. What are they? Drum roll, please! Here they are . . . are you ready?

PRAY OBEY

Are these two words new to me? Of course not! Did I need to hear them again? Obviously I did—I must be a slow learner. In 2002, when I wrote *Back on Track*, the Lord gave me the word "Obey" and the challenge to "Believe, Trust and Obey" for 16 weeks to see what He could do. Well, I finished 12 weeks strong and then floundered for the last 4 weeks, which I wrote about in that book. Why did I flounder those last 4 weeks? I certainly didn't quit believing or trusting God . . . but I definitely quit obeying—just like Peter, when he was walking on the water with Jesus. When he took his eyes off Jesus, Peter began to sink (see Mark 6:45-52).

Here I am six years later, taking a similar challenge. But this time it's different—I've gone from 16 weeks to a year! There is no earthly way I can do this without God's help. The only way I can make it through an entire year is to do what He has told me to do, and write about my experiences as I go. I promise that I'll share with you the good days, the bad days and the in-between days.

I didn't realize it when I woke up this morning hearing the two words "pray" and "obey," but this is exactly what I have been doing the last four days.

On Monday, as I began my one-year journey to *pray* and *obey*, the first thing I did was find a 4x6-inch, ruled index card. I made a list of the deep desires of my heart that could only be fulfilled with God's divine intervention. Only God could do God's part—none of the things on my list were things I could accomplish in a year (or at all!) without Him.

GOD'S PART

If you, then, though you are evil, know how to give good gifts to your children, how much more will your Father in heaven give good gifts to those who ask him!

MATTHEW 7:11

1. Johnny healed from cancer
2. To fulfill God's purpose for my life
3. Our entire family and extended family to know and serve Christ
4. Reach my weight goal and stay there
5. Vibrant health emotionally, spiritually, mentally and physically

If you haven't yet made your "God's part" list, the deep desires of your heart that you'd like to see fulfilled one year from today, I invite you to do so now.

GOD'S PART

If you, then, though you are evil, know how to give good gifts to your children, how much more will your Father in heaven give good gifts to those who ask him!

MATTHEW 7:11

1. _____
2. _____
3. _____
4. _____
5. _____

After I made the list of "God's part," I flipped the card over and made a list of the things I want to do each day for the next year. My list is far from earth-shaking, but it contains all the things I need to do to keep my life in balance—and doing each activity is important if I am to *obey*. I titled this list "My Part":

MY PART

No, I beat my body and make it my slave so
that when I have preached to others, I myself
will not be disqualified for the prize.

I CORINTHIANS 9:27

1. Quiet time, which includes reading my Bible, praying and doing one day of my First Place 4 Health Bible study
2. Exercise every day that I work. Walk at least three miles
3. Start a strength-training program
4. Stay on the food plan and write on my Live-It Tracker
5. Moisturize my face and heels before bed
6. Write in my planner for the next day's work
7. Don't read the paper, book or work a Sudoku puzzle until I have completed the other items on the list

I am thrilled to tell you that for the last four days, I have accomplished everything on my list. The only item I have not done every day is number 3, "Start a strength-training program." I did pray about it though, and on Thursday, my friend Diane Bagby, who is a personal trainer, offered to help me on Tuesdays and Thursdays of each week. (Thursday was my first day to pump iron, but it won't be the last.) I am also praying that God will give me the same love and desire for strength training that I have for aerobic exercise. If I begin to love it, I will be able to incorporate it into my life.

You probably noticed that my to-do list does not contain big-picture desires or needs like what I included on my "God's part" list. Why? Because I know the truth of the founding verse of First Place 4 Health, Matthew 6:33: "But seek first his kingdom and his righteousness, and all these things will be given you as well." My list above is *my part* of the one-year challenge. The list of five things I want to see in my life a year from now is *God's part*. If we are faithful to do our part, He will do His part.

Think about your life and the deep-down desires you've asked God to fulfill one year from today. Are there some things you could begin to do every day that would make *your part* in the situation better? If your marriage is in trouble and you've asked God to restore that relationship, be honest with yourself about what you need to do to begin the healing. Maybe "Quit nagging" needs to be on the list, or "Be an encouragement to my spouse." If your children are the problem, your part could be "Catch my kids doing something good" or "Don't yell." If your finances need God's divine help, you might put on your list "Don't charge anything" or "Don't eat out."

Are you willing to make a list of the things you need to do every day for one entire year with God's help? Remember, these are things that you can do each day, or your part in giving God a year.

After you have had a chance to think and pray about "God's part" and "your part" and feel confident that the items on these lists are the foundation of your year with God, I invite you to make your own card, which you can carry with you all year. On one side, transfer your "God's part" list from above; on the other, copy your "my part" list.

Let me tell you some of the things that have happened during the last four days as I have prayed and obeyed.

As I have prayed for each one of my family members each morning, God has answered my prayers. I am convinced that we don't see more answers because we don't pray. I have been praying that God would strengthen my husband, Johnny, who has stage-4 prostate cancer. For the last month, Johnny has been extremely weak, and I started praying on Monday that

MY PART

No, I beat my body and make it my slave so that when I have preached to others, I myself will not be disqualified for the prize.

I CORINTHIANS 9:27

1. _____

2. _____

3. _____

4. _____

5. _____

6. _____

7. _____

8. _____

God would give Johnny strength. For the last four days, Johnny has felt strong. Each morning when I call him to ask how he feels, I have been astounded to hear him say, "I can tell already this is going to be a good day."

I have been praying this week for our oldest granddaughter, Cara, who is teaching high-school English in a small Texas town. Cara's husband, Michael, has gone back to school full time and is scheduled to graduate next May. They have a two year old, Luke, who is staying with an older lady during the day. Cara asked me to pray for her students and for her each day. She also asked me to pray for Luke in his new surroundings. Well, I am happy to report that Cara has had a really good first week and that Luke has not cried a single morning when Cara has walked him to the door. On

Wednesday, Cara called and asked me to pray for a boy in her class named Kyle. She had noticed on the first day of school that Kyle, a senior, was sullen and withdrawn. He stood outside the cafeteria and refused to go in. On day two, she tried to talk with Kyle but he wouldn't look at her. She asked a teacher next door about him and found out that Kyle is deaf and mute. His mother is also deaf, and his stepfather is a very angry man. Cara said that during lunch she was doing a First Place 4 Health Bible study that I had given her when she was in college. That day's study was about the man who had brought his deaf-mute son to Jesus, and Jesus had healed the boy (see Mark 9:14-32). She told me how when the disciples asked Jesus why they were not able to heal the boy that Jesus said, "This kind of healing only comes through much prayer" (my paraphrase, see v. 29). Cara and I both know that it will take much prayer to break through to Kyle's heart, but our job is to pray. God will do the work to open Kyle's heart.

I am praying for all my children and grandchildren every day, but only God knows the things He wants to do for them this year and what He has already been doing in their lives.

On Wednesday, Vicki Heath was in the office to plan our Wellness Week in October. We always love having Vicki here, but with only one day to work, I prayed that morning that we would be inspired and not spend the morning "chasing rabbits." By 11 A.M., after only two hours, we had the entire week planned. What an answer to prayer.

Obeying has been easy all week. I know it won't always be easy, but I'm glad it hasn't been too difficult so far! The reason it has been easy is that my list of daily activities is achievable—there's no reason *not* to accomplish my short list of daily goals. I also know that if and when I quit obeying, I will start to sink.

I love the new, easier First Place 4 Health food plan. Cheese is now categorized as a milk, and corn and potatoes are now vegetables! Hallelujah! The original food plan was the Diabetes Exchange program. It was a good plan when we began using it in 1981, but today we know so much more about nutrition than we did back then. Not everyone in First Place 4

Health is diabetic, and for those who aren't, the exchange program was sometimes difficult and time-consuming. The new food plan uses the USDA Food Pyramid, which gives excellent guidelines for eating a well-rounded diet and changing from an unhealthy lifestyle to a healthy one. It's also much easier to follow! The new food plan is so easy and fun and after only four days, I am already trying to be sure that I eat different colors of fruits and vegetables each day.

Every day this week, the Lord has sent someone to talk to me while I am walking on the treadmill. I am an extrovert who recharges by being with people, so when someone shows up that I can visit with, the time just flies by. Every day I have been able to finish the entire three miles.

I am full of joy that only comes through obedience. I am fully aware that this is only the first week, but I get so excited when I think of all that God will be able to do if I keep praying and obeying for a year.

A journal is a great tool for keeping up with your progress on giving God a year. There is a journal included in the back of this book to get you started, or you might also consider keeping a record of each day on your computer. I suggest having two sections, the first titled "Pray" and the second "Obey." You decide how best to record your progress: You could write a little every day and then sum up how the week went, or you could write once a week and do a monthly recap. (You can see samples of my "Give God a Year" journal in Appendix A.) However you decide to track your progress, I can assure you that taking a few minutes of honest evaluation will pay rich dividends. If you don't write it down, you're likely to forget all that happens and how God is responding to your prayers and obedience.

2

May the God of hope fill you with all joy and peace as you trust in him,
so that you may overflow with hope by the power of the Holy Spirit.

ROMANS 15:13

I hope you have decided to accept the challenge to give God the next year of your life, but you may still be thinking about what doing so might mean. That's okay—take all the time you need. Time is nothing to God and your year can begin whenever you decide to take the challenge. But for me, I am on board and ready to roll. This morning when I awoke, I was so thankful for how God has orchestrated this adventure in my life, and He will do the same for you if you decide to come along.

This is the commitment for one year: *pray* and *obey*. Not a lot of rules and regulations or dos and don'ts. Because our lives are so different and our needs are not the same, God knows that if we each pray and obey every day for one year, He can do what needs to be done in and through us to make each of our lives sparkle and shine.

If you are a member or leader of First Place 4 Health, God has already given you the group who will be there with you as you take the challenge to give Him a year of your life. If you are not involved in a First Place 4 Health group, I strongly recommend that you find or start one in your community, or connect with another group of people who are seeking for God to change their lives. Support along the journey is important. You don't have to take God's challenge alone.

If you want to know more about the First Place 4 Health program, check out our website, www.firstplace4health.com. (If you put in your zip code, you're likely to find a group meeting close to you—or if there isn't a group close by, you'll find all the tools you need to start one of your own!) Having others in your life to encourage and support you makes a huge difference when you are making difficult lifestyle changes. Although weight loss is the reason many people come to our program, First Place 4 Health is about so much more than losing weight. First Place 4 Health deals with the total person: emotional, spiritual, mental and physical. God seeks our surrender to Him in each part of our lives, and the goal of First Place 4 Health is to give Christ first place in all we do.

First Place 4 Health members learn how to love God in all four areas by breaking up the Christian life into "bite size pieces" that are possible to do each day. In the emotional area, we learn that just because we have emotions, we don't need to act on every one we experience. When we are sad, we can resist eating an entire bag of cookies; when we feel anger, we can avoid screaming at our children or coworkers. Spiritually, we learn how to have a quiet time each day that includes completing one day in a First Place 4 Health Bible study and praying for God's help for that day. We challenge ourselves mentally by memorizing one Bible verse each week so that God can begin changing our thought life, which contains old messages that are not true. Physically, we learn how to eat a healthy diet and how to incorporate regular exercise into our lifestyle. We also learn how important it is to get enough rest and how to manage stress.

The goal is to live a life that is balanced and full of joy no matter what we are going through. A balanced life is the natural by-product of giving Christ first place in every area.

Wherever you go to find encouragement and support for the next year, you may still be thinking that a year is way too long to contemplate—but think about how fast the *last* year has streaked by. Perhaps it's because I am getting older, but it seems like time is literally flying. When Johnny was diagnosed with stage-4 prostate cancer in 1997, he was given a prognosis of one-and-a-half to two years to live. Here we are in 2009, and he is still alive. I am thankful for every day we've had together, yet sometimes it seems like only yesterday that we were getting the doctors' pessimistic forecast. The years have passed so quickly.

Where are you today? Think about the last 10 years and where you might be if you had given God an entire year 10 years ago. What is holding you back from deciding to take the plunge? If it is fear, then begin praying that God will remove your fear so that you might begin with me today. I can tell you that, even though I am only on day six, I am pumped beyond words thinking about what God has planned for me. His plans are for good, not evil, plans to give me hope and a future (see Jer. 29:11).

The storms that come our way in life test where we are with Christ. They point out our level of maturity in our faith and show us where we are weak and need shoring up.

As I write these words, Hurricane Gustav is entering the Gulf of Mexico and is predicted to make landfall between New Orleans and the Texas coast. I have been praying about this storm the last few days, and I know that God knows where we are. We have First Place 4 Health groups in New Orleans and long-time friends there as well. Franklin Avenue Baptist Church has just been rebuilt and it grieves me to think that they might be hit again. We had a First Place 4 Health Conference at this church in April 2005, just four months before Hurricane Katrina devastated the city. We love the people at that church. When I flew to New Orleans the following February to see the city, I was sick about what had happened to that dear church and its people. In June 2006, I heard Elizabeth Luter, the pastor's wife at Franklin Avenue, speak to a group of pastors' wives at our denomination's annual convention. I told her after she spoke, "Elizabeth, you and Fred have earned an A-plus on this test!"

This morning as I prayed, I told the Lord that all we need today is wisdom for whether to start packing or not. The storm is headed for New Orleans, but may turn west—no one knows yet where it may land. My prayer only needs to be for today. *Help me today, then tomorrow help me tomorrow and the next day help me the next day.* Worrying about our future is a futile exercise. The Bible says in Matthew 6:34, "Therefore, do not worry about tomorrow, for tomorrow will worry about itself. Each day has enough trouble of its own."

If you are a worrier (I am not), then you might be worried that if you take this one-year challenge, all kinds of things might happen to keep you from completing the year. Well, my feeling is that if my home is destroyed in the next few days by Hurricane Gustav, then I will be supremely happy that I am safe in the protection of God's love and care because I have com-

30

mitted the next year of my life to Him. He is the One who will see us through, and He is the One who will see all believers through the storm, wherever it hits.

I was praying out loud a couple of days ago as I was driving into Houston, and I couldn't bring myself to pray that the hurricane would not hit here. Instead I prayed, "Lord, Your will be done. Bring glory to Yourself. If Gustav lands here, use this experience for our good and for Your glory." Today, my prayer is that God will do the same for His kids, including you, wherever the storm lands. He is able to lift us up and keep our feet from slipping on a stone, and He is able to help us walk on the water in the middle of the storm.

You might not be a worrier, but you might be a person who feels the need to be in control of your own life. Giving God free reign for the next year might seem like a loss of control to you. I was this kind of person who, even though I had been a believer since I was 12 years old, I thought that I could manage earth and God could manage heaven! It wasn't until I was 42 years old that God was able to break my stubborn will and rebuild the shambles of my life. That controlling nature still wants to rear its head from time to time, but praise God, when I let Him, He runs the ship and I swab the deck.

My prayer is that you will realize today that you have absolutely no control over your own life. We cannot control the circumstances around us, such as whether or not we will have a car accident because someone else chooses to drink and drive. We also can't control the poor choices our spouse or children make. The only thing we have control over are our own actions—how we choose to respond to the circumstances that come our way in our daily life.

I believed a lie for so many years. If I had continued to be the controlling person I was before 1984, could I have stopped the bankruptcy we went through? Could I have prevented Johnny's cancer? Could I have kept a drunk driver from killing our daughter Shari? The answer is a resounding *no!* Praise God, I finally gave up control, and He has been able to do amazing things with my life.

Without God's divine wisdom and help, a control freak is outside the ship paddling hard but going nowhere. Is it possible that the world you inhabit could run just fine without you controlling everything and everyone for one year? Will you consider giving up control of your life and the lives of those you love for one year? Will you let God work on you? God is a perfect gentleman and He will not begin the work that needs to be done in our lives until we give control over to Him.

If control is an issue for you, I ask you to consider praying the prayer I prayed in December of 1984: "Lord, I am not willing, but I am willing to be made willing. Please don't let it hurt too bad." Back then, I was so afraid of what God might do to me if I gave Him control. What a fool I was! He has taken care of me, His daughter, and lifted me higher than I ever deserved to be. Without Him, I could have never survived the shipwrecks of life. But with Him, I have been able to soar during the storm. That, my friend, is what will happen should you decide to take the challenge.

Okay, where are you now? Are you thinking about joining me on this exciting journey? The challenge is to *pray* and *obey* every day for the next year. You pray and ask God for help to do the things on your list. After you pray, you start working on the list. Tomorrow you get up and do it again.

3

ACCEPTING GOD'S LOVE

But God demonstrates his own love for us in this:
While we were still sinners, Christ died for us.
ROMANS 5:8

Matthew 6:33 is the foundational verse for the First Place 4 Health program: "But seek first his kingdom and his righteousness and all these things will be given to you as well." The original name of the program, First Place, was chosen because we believed (and still believe) that if we can learn how to give Christ first place in our lives, He will give us everything we need. The words "4 Health" were added to the name of the First Place program in 2008 because we wanted to bring the four-sided person into the name. Now the name conveys what our program is really about: If I, being a four-sided person—mental, emotional, spiritual and physical—learn how to give Christ first place in my life, then He will give me all the things I need to live a balanced life.

You might be wondering what it means to give Christ first place in all four areas of your life. When I joined the First Place program in 1981, I wondered the same thing. The best way I can explain what this means is to ask you to think about your best friend. You desire to frequently talk with this person to find out how he or she is, and to tell him or her how you are doing. If this friend is sick or in need, you are there by his or her side in a flash. If you have a need, he or she responds in kind. (My mom used to say that when you are an adult, you can count these friends on one hand and still have fingers left over. I have found that statement to be quite true, but I do have a few friends who qualify.)

Women who have this kind of friend want to talk on the phone, shop or have long lunches with this person. They call this person first when they are in "crisis mode." Women who have a person like this in their lives are truly blessed. I call it having someone "with skin on" to share life with.

I'm sure that some men have a best friend they like to hang out with, but my experience with Johnny is that he has me and that's enough. He married me and wants me to be his best friend. Sure, there are guys he likes to talk with about sports or politics, but he doesn't have the need that I do for friends.

I wonder if men don't have more friends because they never had this modeled for them by their own dads. Years ago, before the industrial revolution, men worked at home in the fields. Little boys, by the age of eight or so, began working beside their dads every day. When the boys started school, they still helped Dad milk the cows early in the morning before going to school. Back in those days, boys watched Dad provide for and protect the home. By seeing this on a daily basis, a boy learned how to become a man.

The last book of the Old Testament tells us, "He will turn the hearts of the fathers to their children, and the hearts of the children to their fathers, or else I will come and strike the land with a curse" (Mal. 4:6). I believe we have seen this verse played out in our country today. Today, almost half the homes in America are single-parent homes and Dad is not present on a daily basis. Children need a mother *and* a daddy in the home, and when this doesn't happen there are always consequences.

The home is the first institution God established to be a model of Christ and His church. The husband and father is called to be the head of the home, to provide for and protect his family. The wife and mother is called to be the heart of the home, loving her husband and children. The children are called to learn obedience in the home and to obey because they love their parents so much.

In many homes, this scenario is not modeled or played out. The father might be an alcoholic who neither provides for nor protects his family. The mother might be absent emotionally for the children so they never learn how to properly respond to love. There are many possible situations that can make it difficult for us to grasp the concept that God is our heavenly Father and that He loves us individually, more than anyone else can; Jesus would have been willing to die on the cross if you or I were the only person on earth. If the kind of home you grew up in was far from perfect—and most are—then you might need to begin by asking God to give you tangible evidence of His love.

He might do this by sending someone "with skin on" who loves God and gives Him first place in his or her own life. This person will model for you the kind of friendship God desires to have with you so that you can begin to grasp how much God loves you. We will never become best friends with someone we don't believe loves us.

God also shows us His tangible love when we look at the world He created. Beautiful sunrises and sunsets shout out God's love. Wild flowers bloom in every color and shape. The birds sing of God's tender care, and our pets even model God's unconditional love. He created every kind of wonderful food for us to eat in every imaginable color. How could it be possible for trees to have luscious apples, cherries, pears, lemons and limes if God didn't create them into being?

I have a friend who struggles with knowing that God loves her. God, in His wisdom, has given her the gift of photography, and she frequently emails me the most beautiful pictures, which she takes while out and about in her car. One day she was driving home from dropping her daughters off at school and saw some deer in the trees. She stopped her car and took the most beautiful picture of two deer who blended in perfectly with the trees around them. When I looked at that picture, I knew that God has given her eyes that are tuned to see the beauty of His creation, beauty that would have been hidden from most people's eyes, because He is trying to show His love for her.

God also shows His love in procreation. When we look at the miracle of a newborn baby, we see tangible evidence of God's love and His desire for the earth and its people to continue on. A precious lady in my First Place 4 Health class became pregnant last year and has just given birth to her fourth child at the age of 40. Her other three children are 21, 13 and 8. From the moment I learned of the pregnancy, I knew that this precious woman was being given a very special gift from God to show the entire family how much He loves them. Little Hannah Grace will be such a blessing to this family, and to everyone she meets.

God uses whatever it takes to draw us closer to Him, so if you don't believe God loves you, look around—His love is everywhere.

Jesus calls the church "His bride" (see Rev. 19:7). His desire for you and me is that we desire Him over everything else. We want to talk with Him, be with Him and love Him so much that we would be willing to die for Him—and to live for Him.

This is exactly what it means to give Christ first place in our lives. He wants to become the best friend we have. He wants us to talk to Him frequently and to call on Him when we have good or bad news to share. He wants our thoughts to be about Him during the day. He wants to know our deepest needs and desires. He wants to tell us how much He loves us and know that we believe Him. He wants to give us advice about how to solve our problems and watch us take the advice. Proverbs 18:24 says, "A man of many companions may come to ruin, but there is a friend who sticks closer than a brother." Jesus wants to be the friend "who sticks closer than a brother."

Think about the best friend you have on this earth. This friend disappoints you from time to time because, after all, earthly friends are human. God will never disappoint you or be unavailable when you call. You'll never have to leave a voice message. Your words will go directly to the throne of God. He tells us in Jeremiah 33:3, "Call to me and I will answer you and tell you great and unsearchable things you do not know." God wants to be the friend we call before we even think to call a friend with skin on.

As we learn what it means to love God and to know how much He loves us, we will learn to trust Him to work out the areas of our lives that only He can do.

Learning to love God supremely and to give Christ first place in everything is a process; we will not learn how to do it overnight. That is the main reason that I'm asking you to give God an entire year, a year in which you will *pray* and *obey*. As you do, this kind of friendship will become a reality in your life.

4

If you believe, you will receive whatever you ask for in prayer.

MATTHEW 21:22

One morning in 1990, I learned what it means to really talk to God and have Him talk to me. Before that time, my prayer life consisted of what I like to call "shoot-up prayers," which I shot up to heaven whenever I needed God's help. I knew that intimate prayer was possible because I had gone to every prayer seminar offered at women's retreats, but had no idea how to make communing with God part of my daily life. What was the secret these people knew that I had not discovered? I heard the answer to my question over and over, but for some reason I was simply not able to incorporate the concept of prayer into my life on a daily basis.

The two things I heard in every seminar I attended were always the same: Write your prayers and show up every day to pray. For some reason, I rebelled against these practical pointers; my thinking was that it would take entirely too long to write my prayers—I could talk faster than I could write. And the many times I had "shown up" to pray, I found my mind wandering; instead of praying, I ended up thinking about what I wanted to eat for breakfast or what I was going to do when I got to the office.

That morning in 1990, I decided to try out what I had heard so many times before.

A good friend, Joy, had given me my first journal in 1972. In the front of it, she had written, "For your first book." How could Joy have known that I would ever write a book? We had moved a couple of times between 1972 and 1990, but the journal had moved with us and I knew exactly where it was. I went into the bedroom where the journal resided in a small bookcase. I picked it up and headed to the den with the journal, my Bible and a devotional book, *My Utmost for His Highest* by Oswald Chambers.

That morning is indelibly written on my memory bank. I sat on the sofa in my den and read a devotional to clear my mind and heart. I then read my Bible so that God could speak His Word into my heart. After that, I started writing in the journal—when I finished, I had written four pages. One hour after I had sat down, I got up from the sofa, astounded that an entire hour had passed so quickly. I had finally experienced what so many others before me already knew: God is ready and waiting to have an intimate relationship with us. He wants to be the best friend we will ever have.

For the next seven years, I spent most mornings sitting on the sofa in my den doing the same thing each day. As I wrote my prayers and recorded the answers to my prayers, I had a tangible record of what God was doing in my life. I saw so many answers to prayer that it would take a book to record them all—and that's exactly what my prayer journals became! Today, I can go back to those journals and verify exact dates when God answered my prayers.

This morning, I went to the spot where all my journals are kept and picked up that very first one. Looking through this treasure trove of memories, I was reminded of so many answered prayers and of countless times when God worked in an obvious and miraculous way. Let me share some of these with you.

I read about a time in November 1990, when we were at the retreat at Round Top in central Texas for a First Place Leaders' Retreat. We had 100 leaders there and two keynote speakers. One of the speakers, Diane Nelson, was a soul-winner extraordinaire. Diane had accepted Christ as an adult and was passionate about sharing Christ with everyone she met. As a result of her testimony that weekend, 8 of those 100 First Place leaders asked Jesus into their heart. I was astounded; how could someone leading others in a program based on putting Jesus in first place not know Him personally? That startling experience was God at work; He wanted me to be aware of the possibility that some people in the First Place 4 Health program don't know Him. Because of that revelation, we include the plan of salvation in every one of our Bible studies and also in the *Member's Guide*.

Then I read about and remembered the summer of 1997, when life as I knew it began to change. It is my firm belief that God allows pain and sorrow to come so that He can continue teaching us about Himself and His great love for us. As I look back, I can see God's hand as He orchestrated the events. The summer of 1997 was a busy one. I taught First Place Fitness Weeks for three weeks in Ridgecrest, North Carolina, and for three weeks in Glorieta, New Mexico.

While I was at Ridgecrest, I went to the pay phone (this was before cell phones) to call home. Every night, Johnny talked to me about buying a home on the water. It was very similar to when a man wants to buy a new car: He starts looking at cars all the time. If his wife is resistant to the idea of a new car, he finds ways to bring her around to his way of thinking. He tells her that their car simply is not worth fixing; it is falling apart. You wives know the drill—you are going to be the proud owner of a new car, whether or not you want to be! This "hard sell" is what Johnny was doing every night when I called home, except instead of a car it was a home on Galveston Bay. I was so frustrated that I even asked my group that week to pray that if we had to buy another home, it would be one we could afford!

After I returned home, we did find a little house we could afford, and by the middle of September 1997, we owned a second home.

A month later, we had our annual First Place Wellness Week at Round Top, Texas. Johnny and our two daughters helped with the cooking. Before we left for Round Top, Johnny had some tests to see why he was experiencing some discomfort in his stomach. He had an appointment the Monday after Wellness Week to get the results of and to have some additional tests.

Thursday, on the drive home from Round Top, I received a call from my daughter-in-love, Lisa, saying that their home had burned to the ground. That night, John, Lisa and their three children came to live with us with only the clothes on their backs.

On Monday, we made plans to go to the Bay house after Johnny finished all his bone and CAT scans because we suspected the news would not be good. Our suspicions proved correct: We drove to the Bay that night two broken people. The cancer was stage 4; it was already in Johnny's bones and he likely had only two years to live. As God had planned all along, our little house on the Bay provided shelter that we didn't know would be needed.

On the drive, I was so broken up that I couldn't stop crying. Johnny, on the other hand was not showing any emotion—I'm sure in part because he didn't know what to do with me. Johnny had not eaten all day and was starving, so we decided to stop at a Mexican restaurant for dinner. I was such a wreck that he gave me his sunglasses; we went to a back corner table and I sat facing the wall. Looking back, I have to laugh because I'm sure the staff thought Johnny was a wife-beater because of the way my shoulders heaved as I sat there crying. (I am happy to report that I was able to eat every bite of my supper in spite of my emotional state!)

How could I have known that God had impressed on my husband the urgency of buying that house so that He could move us an hour from Houston to wrap us into a cocoon of His love?

We have been through many difficult times since 1997, but God has held us in His arms every step of the way—and He has used that little house on Galveston Bay to comfort and heal us. My mom came to live with us in 1999, for the last three years of her life. During that heart-wrenching time, I became the parent and she became the child. On occasion, I thought I might die from the heartbreak, but today I am so thankful for the consolation of living just five streets away from the home my parents owned for 20 years on Galveston Bay. I was able to push my mom's wheelchair out onto the pier, where we would sit for several hours each evening. She was totally at peace looking out at the water where years before she had shared so many happy hours.

I read on in my journals. November 22, 2001, was another horrific time when our daughter Shari was struck and killed by a young girl driving drunk. Shari left behind three teenage girls and her husband, Jeff. I believe that when Shari took her first breath, God knew the day He would call her home—but I'm so glad He didn't share that news with me. If He had, I wouldn't have enjoyed a single day of her life. Jeff has done a beautiful job of raising our granddaughters, and our family has seen and experienced God's unfailing love every step of the way on a journey too horrible for words.

I have learned more about God's love and character through the bad times than through the good times (though there have been plenty of those, too!). After Shari's death, I became fearless of what the enemy could do to me. He gave it his best shot when he took Shari from us, but his best shot was only fuel on the fire of my dependence on God.

What if I hadn't gone to the bookcase that morning in 1990 to retrieve the journal given to me in 1972? What if I hadn't learned that a deeper relationship with God was possible? What if Jesus hadn't become the best friend I have in this world? I can tell you what would have happened: I would be one miserable woman today because I would still be trying to run my own life. But because I learned the secret of prayer, I am full of joy and have a hope for the future that no one can quench. I can say unequivocally that my God is able to take care of me until I take my last breath on this earth.

Here's how the "show up" part of the prayer equation has played out in my life. From 1997 to 2008, I lived 46 miles from my job in the First Place 4 Health office. I would arise at 4:00 each morning and leave the house at 5:00 to drive into Houston.

I had a shorter time with God at the house, when I read my Bible and did my Bible study for the day. When I got into the car, I prayed out loud for everything going on in my life. I prayed for each of my family members by name and asked for the specific needs I knew about in their lives. I sat quietly as I drove and listened as God spoke to my heart and instructed me on what I needed to do and who I needed to call.

As for "write your prayers," I use my journal to chronicle specific events going on in my life that need God's intervention or direction. When we moved to the Bay, I could never seem to find a spot to have my time with God. We were in a little cottage in the beginning, and I didn't have a secluded spot where I could be alone. It took a long time for God to show me that there are many ways I can communicate with Him. It can be sitting in my favorite chair or driving in my car. I can talk to Him when I am out for a walk or when I am washing dishes. I make note of these conversations in my journal. Because I learned the discipline of writing my prayers so many years ago, I no longer need to write everything down on paper every day, but the journal is still important because I go back to write the date when God answers and record the circumstances surrounding His answer.

The thing is, we will never learn the joy of praying unless we begin doing it. It's really quite simple: Start showing up each day at the same time, in the same place, and pray. Your prayer life will evolve and change as your circumstances change, but whatever shape it takes, it will become the most precious time of your day. Will you begin praying? Come on, just try it. I promise, you'll never be sorry.

I'll close this chapter by telling you about two specific answers to prayer I have recently received.

The first happened the day I wrote chapter 3. I had gotten up to write at 2:15 A.M., and after writing the chapter on my computer, I saved the file. When I got to the office and restarted my computer, I saw the file, but as I was preparing to send it to Pat's computer, the file disappeared. Lisa, our computer guru, can always find a file that I have lost, but she looked and looked and finally said, "Something is wrong; it's not there." I was frantic, because I had not printed a hard copy of the chapter. I laid my hand on my computer and said, "Lord Jesus, I am going to shut down my computer and when I bring it back up, I am asking You to find this file. I know that You know where it is." When I restarted the computer and opened the book file, there was chapter 3! Minutes before, it was nowhere to be found—but now, it was safe and sound on my hard drive. Lisa and I marveled at what had just taken place. It was obvious to us that our enemy, the devil, did not want this book written and that he would fight me every step of the way. The good news is, he could not win!

The second answer has to do with our oldest granddaughter, Cara. I have been praying two things for Cara each morning. First, that her son Luke will have a great year in child care and, second, that Cara will be set free from her tendency to worry. We have talked together about worry and what a stronghold it can have in our lives. Cara has always been a worrier, but since the death of her mother—our daughter Shari—it has escalated.

Last Saturday, Cara called and said, "You aren't going to believe what happened last night. At dinner, Luke folded his hands and said, 'Pray, okay?'" Cara was surprised because Luke had never done this before. At bedtime, Luke did the same thing, so Cara prayed with him before he went to sleep. Cara thought that the lady keeping Luke must be praying with the children before they eat and before they take their naps; Luke had brought his new habit home.

Cara called again yesterday, and just before we hung up, she told me another amazing story. During the last week, a strange thing has happened. At least four times, she has been in the house thinking and worrying. As she has begun to get "worked up," as she calls it, Luke has yelled out from another part of the house, "Mom, pray!" They have prayed together with his little hands folded in front of him and his little eyes shut. She told me that she has prayed the longest prayers and Luke hasn't moved a muscle until she has said, "Amen." Luke has then said, "Amen," too and then gone on with his playing. Can you see how God is answering my prayers for Cara?

God is using her own two-year-old son to teach her that she can stop worrying! This little boy is being used by God to heal his mom of worry.

What are the greatest needs in your life? Your list of things that only God can do this next year, "God's part," are the starting point for your prayers. If your fractured marriage is number one on your list, then begin your prayers each day asking God for wisdom for what to do or not do, to say or not say, today to begin healing your relationship with your spouse.

If you have a wayward child, pray that God will do whatever it takes to bring your child to Him. Pray that God will send a godly person into your child's life to point him or her to Him.

If your finances are a wreck, ask God to show you ways to cut back on your spending and to miraculously provide the money to pay your bills.

On the top of my "God's part" list, I quoted a favorite Scripture. This verse assures me that God is a better Parent than I could ever hope to be, and that as I obey Him, He will give me the desires of my heart. The verse is Matthew 7:11: "If you, then, though you are evil, know how to give good gifts to your children, how much more will your Father in heaven give good gifts to those who ask him!"

God wants to fulfill the deepest desires of your heart. The five greatest needs you put on your list are not a problem at all for God. Will you begin praying every day for these five things?

Pray, okay?

5

Whoever has my commands and obeys them, he is the one
who loves me. He who loves me will be loved by my Father,
and I too will love him and show myself to him.

JOHN 14:21

On September 9, 2002, I was sitting in my favorite chair in my living room. It was early morning and I was telling God how much I love Him. God had carried me and my family for almost a year since the death of our daughter Shari on Thanksgiving night 2001. I was thanking God for all He had done, when suddenly I was struck by the idea that I didn't have a clue how to love God. I said, "God, I want to love You with my whole heart, but I feel like most of the time I am just scratching the surface."

As I sat there thinking about this, I heard the still, small voice of the Holy Spirit speak into my ear. It was not an audible voice, but I heard it loud and clear in my spirit. The Holy Spirit asked me if I remembered the verse quoted at the beginning of this chapter, John 14:21. Well, of course I remembered it—it was one of my memory verses from the first Bible study I ever completed, back when I joined the First Place program in March 1981.

As I thought about the verse, I had one of those "a-ha!" moments when I suddenly got it. "Oh," I said, "You want me to obey You. That's how I show You I love You." Well, *duh!* God helped me write *Back on Track* during the next four months, based entirely on that one verse. I lost 16 pounds during 16 weeks of getting back on track—but here I am again, needing to lose the same 16 pounds again. Now, instead of 16 weeks, God has asked me for an entire year. Obviously, I didn't fully get what it means to show God how much I love Him by obeying Him, so now I'm getting a "do-over" of the lesson.

How many times have we repeated the same lesson over and over because we didn't get it the first (or the second or third!) time? This has been true for me in so many areas of my life. Every time I have had a do-over, it's because I haven't yet learned how to consistently obey God. God has good plans for my life and for yours, but He must have our cooperation—in the form of obedience—to complete those plans.

There was a time when I was conscious of my disobedience but it didn't bother me a whole lot. Of course, I knew it was wrong, but I was controlled by me and me alone. Even though I had become a Christian at the age of 12, I was still willful and headstrong. Today, I am no longer consciously rebellious and willful, but still I disobey. Why is this?

I believe there are several reasons that we don't consistently obey God's will for our lives. These reasons are not all that complex. Life just gets in the way and before we know it, we are once again paddling our canoe with one oar. That one oar symbolizes me in control. When I have two oars, I have God helping me go forward instead of just going around in circles.

What are some of the reasons we stop obeying?

1. We Stop Meeting with God to Receive Our Orders for the Day

As humans, we are inclined to do our own thing, failing again and again to do God's thing. This failure is often due to our neglect of time with God to find out what God's thing is. When I forego my time with God each morning, I act on the belief that I can do life by myself. Our *excuses* are varied—we oversleep, have a sick child or just don't feel like taking the time—but the real *reason* is self-centeredness instead of God-centeredness.

When we take time to pray and ask God for help and guidance during the day ahead, we become conscious of His presence all day long. When we are tempted to lose our temper, God's Spirit prompts us to be kind. When we have a problem at work or at home, God's Spirit helps us solve it.

When we don't take time, however, a downward spiral is set in motion. The longer we miss our time with God, the farther from His presence we feel. As we begin to feel displaced, the desire to meet with Him diminishes and is replaced by other desires. When the desire has been replaced, it's easy to believe that the busyness of life is more important than spending time with God. We begin to feel as if God is far away and we can never go back to where we once were.

Nothing could be farther from the truth. God is teaching me that He never intended for me to do this thing called obedience by myself. Without His help, I am doomed to fail. I've heard it said that 80 percent of life is just showing up. If that is true, my job is to show up to meet with God, whether I feel like it or not. God will restore me and help me every time I turn to Him, no matter how far down the spiral I descend—just like the Israelites' wandering in the wilderness (see Exod. 16:35). Without God, I continue to wander, but with God, I head toward the Promised Land, where I can do the "God thing" I am called to and created for.

2. We Are Not Intentional on a Daily Basis

It has been said that when we fail to plan, we plan to fail. For this reason, I carry my index card with me wherever I go, as a reminder of the activities I've decided to do as "my part" every day. I have planned in advance to accomplish each item, instead of just "hoping" that somehow things will change:

MY PART

No, I beat my body and make it my slave so that when I have preached to others, I myself will not be disqualified for the prize.

I CORINTHIANS 9:27

1. Quiet time, which includes reading my Bible, praying and doing one day of my First Place 4 Health Bible study
2. Exercise every day that I work. Walk at least three miles
3. Start a strength-training program
4. Stay on the food plan and write on my Live-It Tracker
5. Moisturize my face and heels before bed
6. Write in my planner for the next day's work
7. Don't read the paper, book or work a Sudoku puzzle until I have completed the other items on the list

The items on my list include much of what I have learned through the First Place 4 Health program. I want to pray every day, read my Bible and complete one day of the First Place 4 Health Bible study. I want to practice my memory verses every day. I want to walk three miles every day that I work at the office—by doing this, I am assured of exercising at least four days every week. I want to complete my Live It Tracker every day so that I can be accountable to my First Place 4 Health group for my eating and exercise habits.

Let me make an admission: I have taken many time-management classes. I have owned four different day-planners, thinking each time I bought a new one that *this* time would be different. The problem with all those planners is that I was never intentional about writing in them, and the problem with the classes is that I was never intentional about using what I learned. A balanced life is only possible if I am intentional about doing what needs to be done on a daily basis, so writing in my planner is on my list of daily activities.

I included strength training on my list because I don't like it—but I desperately need to do it. As we age, we lose muscle tone and strength. Even though my lower body is strong, my upper body needs additional help to be strong as well. The only way I will maintain a strong and healthy body is to be intentional about giving it what it needs.

The beauty of being intentional is that once you have written down what you want to accomplish, you are much more inclined to remember it. And besides that, it's just so much fun to check off your tasks when you're done!

As I said in an earlier chapter, the list above is *my* part of the year I've given over to God—these are the things I do to obey Him. By being intentional on a daily basis, I show the Lord how much I love Him. As I obey, God is able to open up the windows of heaven and shower me with blessings too many to enumerate, including the blessing of seeing my five desires for the year fulfilled.

From time to time, people say to me that "First Place 4 Health is just not working for me anymore. I'm not losing weight and my life is upside down again." As I begin asking them questions such as, "Are you having your quiet time?" or, "Are you exercising?" I always hear the same answer: "No, I'm not."

Success in any area means accepting three facts:

1. God gives us strength to do the hard work.
2. Others encourage us to do the hard work.
3. We are the only ones who can do the hard work.

We tend to get those three facts mixed up. We want God to do the hard work. Or we isolate ourselves when we are struggling so that no one is there to encourage us. In Alcoholics Anonymous, "insanity" is defined as "doing the same thing over and over and expecting a different result." If we're not accomplishing *our* part of our year with God, why would we expect our lives to change? We must do the hard work.

Each day is a new beginning, a fresh slate to begin again. Begin the day with God and then be intentional by doing your part. I promise that as you do, God will do His.

6

You know my folly, O God; my guilt is not hidden from you.

PSALM 69:5

I hope that you've already made your two lists. The first list is the five things you want to see made a reality in your life one year from now. This is *God's* part of the year you have given to Him. The second list is of the tasks you will do every day for the next year. This is *your* part. God will work on the first list in answer to your obedience to the second. Your obedience frees God's hand to show Himself strong on your behalf.

I have many favorite Bible verses, but the one above is not among them. Psalm 69:5 is not a verse I quote to encourage myself; it is always a confession for me that comes to mind on occasions when I have stepped out of God's perfect will for my life.

What is God's will for my life and how can I know it? Micah 6:8 pretty well sums up what God requires of you and me: "He has shown you, O man, what is good. And what does the Lord require of you? To act justly and to love mercy and to walk humbly with your God."

Let's take a closer look at the three components of God's will for us.

Act Justly

To act justly just means to do what is right. And as Psalm 69:5 reminds me, God knows my folly on this one.

It is right to obey the laws of the land, and I have a real problem obeying the speed limit. Driving more than 100 miles each day increases the likelihood that I will exceed the speed limit from time to time. Actually, it's more than time to time—I have received a number of speeding tickets over the years, and even more since we moved to Galveston Bay.

In Texas, you are allowed to take a defensive driving course to keep a speeding ticket from appearing on your permanent driving record. This course is six hours of the most boring instruction possible, and there is no way to get around the six hours required. I have had the joy of completing the course seven times in the last ten years! I have taken the course by DVD in my own home five times and twice attended a class where a comedian presents the material.

The amazing thing is that I seem to be able to go an entire year without getting a ticket. You can only take the course once a year, which proves that I have the ability to act justly by not driving too fast.

This year has been one to top all the others, and I will not soon forget what God is trying to teach me. My year was up in December and I began to wonder when I would get my next ticket. It happened in January.

Shortly thereafter, I was having lunch with a friend. When I told her about the ticket, she told me that she knew an attorney in town who would "take care" of the ticket for $100. Now, I knew that hiring someone to fix my mistake was not something I should do, but it sounded so much easier than the six-hour defensive driving course. So I got the name of the attorney and hired him to "take care" of my ticket.

God had other plans.

The attorney asked for a jury trial and the court date was set months out from the actual ticket. The first time I was to appear in court was the day after Memorial Day. I showed up in traffic court at 8:15 A.M. and sat there while they called all 100 names in the room. After roll call had happened twice and my name had not been called, I went up to the front to inquire about the reason. My court date had been rescheduled to July 15. There were a couple of problems. First, the attorney had not let me know about the rescheduling and, second, I would be at the annual Christian booksellers' convention on July 15.

When I returned to my office, I called the attorney to explain that I would be unable to go to court on July 15, only to be told that I had to be there. My only other option was to write a really sad letter to the judge to request a rescheduling of my court date. I wrote the letter and included copies of my plane ticket and hotel reservation. Several weeks later, I received notice that my plea had been rejected. When I called the attorney, it was suggested that I try again by writing an even more pitiful letter. I did so, and my plea was rejected a second time. The attorney said that my only other alternative was to post an $80 bail—he would go to court and post bail on July 15 so that a warrant would not be issued for my arrest!

Can you see how deep this is getting? It doesn't stop there.

My hearing was rescheduled for a date in August. I ended up spending the entire day in that courtroom only to be told at the end of the day that they would not be able to get to my case and would need to reschedule. I was rescheduled for a couple of weeks later—and this time it was at a downtown courthouse where the parking was $16 a day.

After two hours in court on the appointed day, my case was finally dismissed. By that time, I had promised God that if He would have mercy on me for this foolish act, I would never do it again.

The friend who referred me to the attorney has been astounded by what I've gone through to "take care" of this ticket, but I have not been surprised at all. I heard a speaker say one time, "Others may; you cannot." Others may try to avoid eating their just desserts; those who claim to follow Christ cannot. God wants to teach me this lesson once and for all because He cares about me and wants to keep me, and the other people on the highway, safe.

What is the problem? I drive too fast. What is the solution? Slow down and obey the law. Put my car on cruise control and stop speeding.

Acting justly includes more than correcting the wrongs we do; it also means doing the right thing when it's time to do it. God knows my folly in this area as well. In 1984, when my husband lost his forklift business and we were forced to declare bankruptcy, I was about as low as I had ever been. I was so despondent over our situation that I didn't file our taxes for three years. I thought about it constantly, but just couldn't seem to muster the strength to get it done.

One day, inevitably, I received a letter in the mail with "IRS" stamped on the return side of the envelope. I opened the letter to read that I had exactly one week to turn in my taxes for the last three years. If I had acted justly—by filing my taxes on time, in spite of my depression—I would have saved myself and Johnny additional stress. But I didn't do the right thing when it was time to do it. God helped me, as He always has, to get all three years' returns completed in one week—but it would have been much easier if I had done the right thing when it was time to do it.

What about you?

Do you continually do or say things that make your life more difficult? What action steps can you take to take off the pressure? Do you buy cookies for the kids, but then eat them all on the way home? Stop buying the cookies! Does your spouse get hurt or angry every time you say _____? Why not just stop saying it?

Or are you *not* doing something that needs to be done, something that, every day you put it off, is becoming a bigger and bigger headache for tomorrow? Do you know you need to exercise but never do? Make an appointment three times a week and keep it. Do you want to have a quiet time with God but haven't started? Gather your Bible, a study and your journal and set your alarm tonight to meet with Him tomorrow morning. Do you eat out all the time and ruin your intentions to eat healthy? Find a few nutritious, delicious, easy-to-prepare recipes in a book or online and go to the grocery store.

Why not sit down and write in your journal the mistakes you make again and again that keep you from "acting justly." After you make the list, write beside each thing an action statement that will help you stop the destructive behavior. Then make a list of the good things you want or need to do, and beside each item write an action statement that will help you begin "acting justly."

Even small changes can seem like hard work, but remember the three facts we discovered in the last chapter:

1. God gives us strength to do the hard work.
2. Others encourage us to do the hard work.
3. We are the only ones who can do the hard work.

You can do it! Begin acting justly today, and you will take the first step toward a life of obedience.

Love Mercy

My dear friend Pat Lewis has shown me a lot of mercy over the years. Pat and I were working together when I got that letter from the IRS, and she offered to take a week's vacation to help me file the returns. The first year's return went quickly because I had kept good records, but the other two were much more difficult—we had to reconstruct the books from the checks alone. It took the entire week to get this big job done, but in the end, we got money back for each of the three years so we didn't owe a penalty for filing late. God showed so much mercy during those days, but He also used those hard times to humble me so that I would begin to depend on Him instead of myself.

Putting off unpleasant tasks is something we all do from time to time, but I am a master at this. When my mom moved in with us in 1999, we sold her condo and took the boxes with all her things to our house on the Bay. Those boxes stayed in a huge closet in our home for nearly 10 years—I just couldn't find the strength to go through them. I didn't put sorting the boxes on the list of "my part" tasks because I knew I wasn't going to tackle it every day, but God in His mercy brought the circumstances together. When we were preparing for Hurricane Gustav, my precious girls helped me go through every box. Now it's done.

We all love mercy when it is shown to us, but how many times do we show mercy to those around us? God, my family, my friends and my co-workers have shown me mercy in countless situations, and I have a responsibility to show mercy to those I come in contact with each day.

When you think about your life, I'm sure there are people who come to mind who have shown you mercy on countless occasions. It might be a parent, your spouse or your boss—but it most certainly is God. Jesus said in Luke 6:36, "Be merciful, just as your Father is merciful." God is full of mercy for us, and is always ready to show mercy when we need it.

Is there someone who needs you to show them mercy today? As we begin to love mercy, we show mercy to those who seemingly don't deserve it. This includes those who cut us off in traffic or those who speak rudely for no reason. Jesus said in Luke 6:27-28, "But I tell you who hear me: love your enemies, do good to those who hate you. Bless those who curse you, pray for those who mistreat you." We are called to show mercy even to those who hurt us.

To start becoming a person who loves mercy, make two lists in your journal: the first of all the people you can think of who show you mercy, and the second of all the people who need mercy from you. Next to each name, write specific actions that are a demonstration of mercy. Pray through the first list of names, thanking God for the mercy shown to you. Then pray through the second list, asking God for strength to show mercy, even when it's difficult.

Finally, consider making new lists each month of people who have shown you mercy and of people in need of mercy. As you journey through your year with God, you'll watch yourself becoming a person who loves mercy.

Walk Humbly with Your God

When we "act justly and love mercy," it is a natural progression to "walk humbly with our God." Walking through life in humility simply means that we never take credit for anything good that happens in our life. We know that it is only by God's mercy and grace that we accomplish anything good, and that without Him we can do nothing.

All of us will battle our flesh until the Lord Jesus comes to take us home. Our flesh only wants to please itself. Our body wants to eat what it wants to eat. We want credit for what we do. We want others to love and respect us and tell us how wonderful we are.

Recently, my feelings were hurt by someone I count as a friend. A couple of things were said that compounded the hurt, and before I knew it, I found myself getting angry. I let out my anger to Pat, who is also friends with this person; I just knew she would sympathize with me. But instead, Pat said, "You know you will have to forgive her." I immediately shot back, "I know . . . but not today!"

The next morning in my quiet time, I asked God to forgive me. And I forgave my friend. Walking humbly with God means that I forgive the slight and forget about it. I go on as though nothing has happened because my friend doesn't even know that she hurt me. It isn't necessary for me to tell her about the hurt because it was not intentional—and even if it was, it is not my place to change her; it is God's place to change all of us. His desire is for me walk humbly with Him. This means not clinging to my rights or demanding that others pay for what they do, even when it hurts my feelings.

It has been said that there are three great fears in life:

1. Loss of face
2. Loss of place
3. Loss of life

When we get our feelings hurt or demand our rights from others, it usually stems from one of these three fears. In my story above, my anger was the result of fear number 2, a "loss of place" in my friend's life. When I got my own heart right, this fear dissolved and I was able to walk again in humility with God.

I suggest writing in your journal about the three fears above. In what areas of your life are you afraid of "losing face" (being ashamed), "losing place" (being rejected) or "losing life" (yours or a person's you love)? After you write about your fears, write a prayer asking for God's help in alleviating them, acknowledging that fear focuses our attention on ourselves and not on God. We cannot walk humbly with God when our focus is on ourselves.

Most of us need some help learning how to walk humbly with God, and we can find the help we need in God's Word. Philippians 2:3 says, "Do nothing out of selfish ambition or vain conceit, but in humility consider others better than yourselves." Another great verse is found in Matthew 23:12: "For whoever exalts himself will be humbled, and whoever humbles himself will be exalted."

Our God knows that when we only do what we want to do, we are miserable and will never accomplish His purposes for our lives. Therefore, He allows circumstances into our lives that can teach us, if we are willing, how to act right, how to give and receive mercy and how to walk with Him in humility. He is waiting for us to invite Him in. God knows our folly and wants to change us from the inside out, but we must first recognize that we have a problem and ask for help.

I live my life by one simple phrase: *Do the next right thing.* It's a simple phrase, but it is a powerful reminder of God's will for my life: to act justly, love mercy and walk humbly with Him every day.

Are you ready and willing to do the next right thing?

7

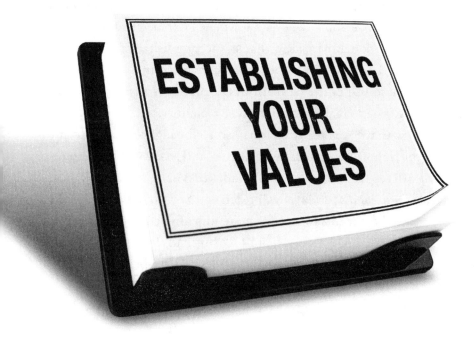

ESTABLISHING YOUR VALUES

For physical training is of some value, but godliness has value for all things, holding promise for both the present life and the life to come.

1 TIMOTHY 4:8

Several years ago, God brought a woman into my life who was younger than any of my children. We became instant friends, and as we got to know each other better, I discovered that Becky was, without a doubt, the most organized person I had ever known. As I watched Becky plan her work and then work her plan, I saw that she accomplished far more than I did. Becky used a day-planner, but I had convinced myself that I just wasn't the type to use one. The truth of the matter is that no one had ever taken the time to teach me how to use a planner.

God knew that I was ready to learn, so He brought Becky into my life at just the right time. One day when Becky and I were working out together, she offered to teach me how to plan. Becky said, "If you will meet with me at 6 A.M. each Monday, I will teach you how to use a planner." I agreed, and we began to call our Monday morning time together our "9/27 meeting." This name came from 1 Corinthians 9:27 which says, "I beat my body and make it my slave, so that when I have preached to others, I myself will not be disqualified for the prize."

The first thing Becky helped me with was to establish my values. She showed me her list of values, and each week after that, she asked if I had made my own list. One morning when she asked and I still hadn't done it, she said, "Let's do it right now." She sat patiently as I made my list, and I was amazed that it didn't take nearly as long as I had thought it would.

The reason for making a list of what you value most in life is so that you can plan your work based on what you value and let go of anything else. Your list of values might not look anything like mine, but there is no right or wrong when it comes to this list. Do you value time alone with your spouse? Would you like to have a better relationship with your children? If these are your values, then you will make the time in your schedule for them.

Here is my values list:

Carole Lewis
January 1, 2008

Values

1. *Godliness.* I want to live my life so that when others think of me, the word "godly" comes to mind. To do this, I must spend time each day reading, studying and memorizing the Bible. I must endeavor to give Christ first place in all I do at work, home and play.

2. *Encourager.* I want to encourage everyone I meet. I will never "trash can" anyone, because God loves them as much as He loves me. I will always try to use Scripture to encourage others, knowing that only God's Word can truly change a life.

3. *Integrity.* I will endeavor to be the kind of person who tells the truth in love. I will not lie or steal. I will always speak good of my brothers and sisters in Christ.

4. *Model excellence.* I will live my life in such a way that I model excellence in all I do. I will give it my all when I work each day, spending the morning hours working, when I am most productive. I will lead in an excellent manner, living my life so that others can follow me, knowing they will succeed.

5. *Family first.* I will give my family first place after God. This means I will spend time with them on birthdays and special occasions. I will call and email on a regular basis.

6. *Friends.* I will take the time to be with the friends God gives me. I will ask God to give me new friends who inspire me to keep growing. I will ask God to help me be that kind of friend also.

7. *Maintain a strong and healthy body.* I will eat only foods that build good cells in my body. I will eat unhealthy foods rarely or never. I will exercise my body every day that I work. I will do aerobic exercise, strength training and stretching as part of my exercise routine.

8. *Financially independent.* I will stay debt-free. I will trust God to give us the money to give back to Him. I will give 10 percent of all I earn to my church. I will ask God to show me how to retire and be financially solvent.

Becky had been working with me for months before she finally made me write down my values. I suggest that this be the first thing you do, because everything else flows out of what you truly value in life. It is important for you to know what you value in life before you, with God's help, can begin the process of bringing order to the chaos. Your values are *your* values, so don't worry about how they look to someone else. If you want something to be one of your values but it isn't right now, then write it down as though it already is.

When Becky offered to help me, she told me to purchase a planner with two pages per day. The left side is for my tasks and the right side is for notes. I giggled as I purchased my fifth planner, but this time proved to be very different from the others; now I had someone to help me learn how to use it.

When I bought my fifth planner, I got one with the cheapest binder available. It was plastic and a burgundy color that I really didn't like at all,

68

but because I had failed so many times, it didn't make sense to me to spend money on a nice binder. It wasn't long before I regretted that decision, but our God specializes in giving us the desires of our hearts: One day while shopping in a resale shop in Ventura, California, I picked up a Brighton brown leather binder that had a price tag of 95 cents! This binder retails for $250, and I would have never spent that kind of money; but God blessed me with a binder that was not only useful but beautiful as well.

Each Monday morning, we sat down with my planner and my calendar and looked at my week. We wrote all the meetings and appointments on each day. Then Becky would ask me, "What would you like to accomplish this week?" When I answered the question, she would ask me which day would be a good one to get the job done.

For instance, one week I wanted to clean out my closets and take all my unwanted clothes to the mission. I had clothes in every closet in our home except Johnny's. I had two closets full of clothes in my Mom's old room, and the other two bedroom closets were stuffed, too. My own closet, which was a large walk-in, was overflowing. Some of these clothes hadn't been worn in years, while others were lost because I didn't know which closet they were in.

Becky suggested that every Monday night for the next few weeks, I spend just 15 minutes going through one of the closets. I was to take out any unwanted clothes and put them in my car. On Tuesday morning, I would drive over to the mission and drop off the clothes. This was something I could do, and I was excited that first Monday to get started! And I was doubly delighted that it only took a couple of weeks to get a mountain of clothes delivered to the mission. The fun part was that I was able to donate many beautiful suits to our Christian Women's Job Corp program. These suits were given to women when they finished their training and went out to interview for a job.

A friend once told me how to eat an elephant: one bite at a time. One of the reasons we never get started is that the task is too big to tackle in the middle of an already busy life. If we break the task into bite-sized pieces, however, we can get it done.

My fun-loving personality does not lend itself to structure and order. I never could bear the idea of eating roast, potatoes and carrots every Sunday. I love change and adventure so much that the thought of a structured, predictable life was always something I thought of as boring and dull. For many years, this way of thinking kept me from learning that there is another way to live life than the way I'd always done it.

My distaste for orderly living goes back many years. I remember, when I was a young wife and mother, having the electricity turned off because I had forgotten where I put the bill. Years ago, the light company used to send a warning slip before shutting service down, but I would periodically misplace the warning slip and one of the utilities would be shut off—which caused more work than if I had just taken the time to pay the bill. I look back on those days in disbelief that I could have lived with such a high level of disorder. I share this with you because your life might look a lot like mine did back then.

After I joined First Place in 1981, I started to realize that my life lacked any kind of order. Dottie Brewer, the founder of First Place, taught time-management classes, which I attended four times over a period of years. I was amazed at the order in Dottie's life. She kept a notebook that contained everything she might ever need to know. The notebook was always in her possession. If Dottie was at the store and needed fluorescent lights, she looked in the notebook to see what size she needed. If she was buying gifts, she looked under her child's tab to see what they wanted. I was fascinated, but I totally misunderstood the teaching I heard from Dottie: I thought there was some kind of power in that notebook of hers, so each time I took Dottie's class, I bought a new notebook! I decided that I must have the wrong color or that I didn't have the right tabs, because I had only used the last one for sermon notes.

This lack of order played out in every area of my life. I never had a consistent prayer time because I didn't plan for it. I didn't have a place where my Bible, Bible study and devotional book would always be when I showed up. By the time I finished hunting for all my tools, I was out of the mood.

God began working on this area of my life shortly after I joined First Place. While I was busy attending time-management classes, God knew I had desperate need for a more ordered life, and that need called for drastic measures. In 1984, we found ourselves in desperate financial straits. For 20 years, I had had the money to pay the bills, but I was too disorganized to do a good job of it. We tithed sporadically but never consistently. Our credit was not good because bills were paid late. Now we found ourselves without the money and with the same problems—and more.

I was sick and tired of my disorganization and disordered life. In December 1984, when I was at my lowest point, I finally gave up the reins of my life to God. I just knew that it was going to be the most painful thing ever. I also knew that I was in a mess and that only God could help me get out of it.

I am amazed today at how God took over in our greatest time of need. We started tithing 10 percent of our income in January 1985, and have continued the habit to this day. I found it easier to tithe when we didn't have much than when we had a lot. The secret, we discovered, is to pay God first, not with what we have left over.

We started paying our bills on time. In the beginning, we had to call our creditors and settle on an amount we could pay each month. As we met our obligations month after month, we were able to get out of debt and begin to establish a good credit rating.

God was at work, bringing order out of chaos. Over the years, He has given us far more than we deserve and taken care of us financially. I believe He has done so because I gave Him permission to come into this area of my life.

I never realized how my lack of order in the financial area spilled over into every area of my life. As we got our finances in order, I also found it easier to establish a regular quiet time each day. God was bringing order out of chaos.

My life had improved dramatically, but God still had work to do to make me into the woman He designed me to be. I became the director of First

Place in 1987, and the program grew from 50 churches using the program to over 1,200 churches in 1990. I take no credit for this rapid growth; it was all God's perfect timing to do what He had prepared in advance to do.

I was much younger back then and was able to keep many tasks on track without writing them down. Even though I could do this, it was exhausting to have to continually remember what needed to be done. As I have gotten older, remembering everything has become increasingly harder—the details might not come back to my mind in time to make a difference. Another problem with not writing down what needs to be done is that I did most of it myself and never delegated the workload to someone else.

On September 13, 2008, Hurricane Ike brought unbelievable chaos (see the photos on the following page), but God has brought order and a peace I would have never believed possible. We lost our lovely home and all our furniture and possessions. The task that now lies ahead is simply to wait until God shows us the next step to take. We don't have a clue what the next step is, but we are at peace in the confidence that God is committed to bringing order out of the chaos of our lives.

How grateful I am that my girls took all the family pictures the week before when we thought Gustav might be headed our way. I'm also grateful that all those clothes were at the mission instead of in Galveston Bay. But I am most grateful that God invited me to spend a year with Him just three weeks before Hurricane Ike came ashore. He knew I would need to be snuggled up real close to withstand the kind of disaster that completely upturned the life we once knew.

When Hurricane Ike landed, our lives changed drastically overnight. The storm surge that accompanied Ike destroyed our home and took every possession we owned, depositing them in Galveston Bay. Because God knew this event was going to happen, He had already been preparing me through Becky. By the time the storm came, I knew how to use my planner, but I still didn't know all the planner could do to help me.

Becky came up to The Retreat at Round Top, where we stayed for five weeks after the storm. She showed me how to make a tab in my planner for

Hurricane Ike. Every name and phone number related to the disaster is in this section. Every date when an adjuster came, along with their contact information, is listed. That tab has become an indispensable tool. We were required to make a list of every piece of furniture, clothing and literally every item that was in our home. My daughter Lisa set up a spreadsheet in the Excel program on my computer, and we began making lists, room by room. This was a huge task, but it was made so much easier by the organizational skills I had learned with Becky's help.

There is much to be said for simplifying our lives. Although I wouldn't have chosen this method, it has been nice to make three moves in the last three months without needing to rent a truck. God has taken care of our every need. For five weeks, we were at Round Top with absolutely everything provided. We left with all our worldly possessions loaded in my car and Johnny's truck—and most of the bulk was the two cat carriers, a birdcage and our dog, Meathead!

We rented our next-door neighbor's home at the Bay for two months following the storm, and were able to take care of the details of tearing down our home and meeting with all the insurance adjusters. After all that was done, we moved back to Houston for the winter, where God has provided a lovely townhouse that belongs to our friend Linda. Linda had bought a new home, but didn't feel she could move until she sold her townhouse. When I asked if she might want to rent it, she was thrilled because she could now move and not have the expense of two houses. Linda left it completely furnished, so we moved one more time in two vehicles.

I can honestly say that, since Hurricane Ike, we have not wanted for a single thing that God has not provided.

Could this be your year to establish your values and begin bringing order out of the chaos of your life? If this is one of the things you put on "God's part" of your card, it was probably because you know that it is not humanly possible for you to accomplish without God's intervention.

Do you really desire for God to bring order out of the chaos of your life? Why not give God a year and change your life forever? Pray and ask

Before Hurricane Ike

After Hurricane Ike

God to send you a "Becky" to help. Becky tells me that "we will not change until the pain is great enough." Is the chaos of your life painful enough to turn it over to God? He will be faithful to help you change permanently for the better, ordering your life in ways that you have scarcely imagined.

Begin by making a list of the most important areas of your life where chaos reigns. Is it your home, your car, your finances? Is it the behavior of your children or your spouse? Begin praying over these areas every day, asking God for help to bring order out of the chaos.

Then begin taking baby steps in whatever ways you can. Could you spend 15 minutes per week sorting through the mess? You might be surprised how much you can accomplish in just a few minutes—sometimes avoiding a task makes it seem much larger than it actually is!

If the chaos involves family members, it may be that you must stop enabling their bad behavior. For instance, if your children just can't seem to get their dirty clothes into the hamper, perhaps you should stop doing it for them. Wash only the clothes that make it to the laundry. After a few weeks of wearing unwashed clothes, it's likely your kids will be more than happy to put dirty duds where they belong!

When there is no order and chaos reigns, it affects not only us; it affects everyone in the family. Pray and obey for a year. God will bring order out of the chaos of your life.

8

No temptation has seized you except what is common to man. And God is faithful;
he will not let you be tempted beyond what you can bear. But when you are
tempted, he will also provide a way out so that you can stand up under it.

1 CORINTHIANS 10:13

We all know the progression. It begins with a thought, which when entertained, proceeds to an action. It really doesn't matter what the temptation is, the end result is always the same: Once we give in to the temptation, we find ourselves in a mess one more time.

Here is a truth we must acknowledge: We will never be free from temptation. But if temptation is to be an ever-present problem for us, how will we ever succeed in our quest for a better life? Some of us have failed to resist temptation so many times that we now believe we will never be any different. This is faulty thinking that is not rooted in the Word of God.

Jesus was as human as you and me, yet He was without sin. How did He resist temptation? He used the Word of God and the power of God's Spirit to resist the devil's schemes. He got up very early to meet with His Father to receive strength for the day ahead. He knew what the Word of God said and was able to quote it to Satan when He was tempted.

Is there any hope for our success unless we do the same thing?

For me, the problem lies in the fact that I don't pray and ask for God's strength when I am tempted. I've already eaten whatever I've eaten or said whatever I've said before I stop, think and pray.

I have had success in the eating area of my life for two of the last six months. Now, I have not totally floundered, but for two months I was successful in not eating desserts. During those two months, everything else went smoothly as well. Kind of reminds me of the founding verse of First Place 4 Health: "But seek first his kingdom and his righteousness, and all these things will be given you as well" (Matt. 6:33). When I stopped seeking to gratify my sweet tooth and started seeking God first, all four areas of my life—physical, mental, emotional and spiritual—came into balance.

Temptation is not limited to overeating, even though this area of temptation leads to the kind of mess that shows on the outside of our bodies. Temptation can come in the form of anger at something unkind said to us. Or it can come when we become aggravated with someone over something done (or not done) again and again, such as not taking out the trash or leaving clothes lying all over the house. We build up a head of steam, and before we know it, we have said much more than the incident deserves.

We might find ourselves tempted to cultivate inappropriate friendships, which could eventually lead to infidelity and divorce. Or we might be tempted to indulge in Internet pornography, which distorts sexuality, dishonors our spouse and corrupts our view of ourselves.

We might be tempted to overspend or charge excessive amounts on credit cards that we cannot pay when the bill arrives, digging ourselves ever deeper into the hole of debt.

God uses circumstances in our lives to show us that we are not strong enough to resist temptation in our own strength. Without God's strength, we are all doomed to failure. So what is the way out when we are tempted? I believe that our way out of temptation comes from the Holy Spirit, who lives inside every believer. He is the one who will help me say no to overeating, to retaliating with unkind words and to exploding over the daily aggravations of life. He is the one who can and will help us overcome temptations to overspend or to dishonor our spouse.

The secret, I have found, is in understanding how temptation works. Our enemy, the devil, can't read our minds, but he knows how we have responded to temptation in the past. He sets up the same scenarios and waits for us to fall back into our old patterns of behavior.

On August 24, 2008, when I decided to give God a year, I knew it would not be easy. I knew my weaknesses, and I knew that I would probably have to write about my failings as they came along so that you, the reader, might see that there is absolutely no temptation that is not common to man (or woman). Here goes . . .

I had three great weeks with the Lord before Hurricane Ike landed and destroyed our home and all our possessions. Even the week after Ike was good, because I continued to lean on God for strength. Week five was when the trouble began. We were staying at Round Top in the Texas hill country, surrounded by people who love us. Our daughter Lisa and her husband, Kent, were there with us because they had no electricity in their home. Lisa cooked nutritious, healthy meals the entire time she was there.

So where did the trouble begin? How did the temptation come?

A long-time friend came to the retreat center with a group from her church. They had expected eight couples, but only three were able to come because of the hurricane. My friend had cooked for weeks to have enough food for the weekend and had a mountain of leftovers. When she was ready to return to Houston, she brought all the food over to the house where we were staying, and gave it to us. You might be thinking, *What a nice thing for her to do.* But when I saw the food she brought in, I knew it might be a problem for me. Along with the lunchmeat and bread were cookies and all kinds of desserts.

What was my way out? Get it out of the house! Did I do that? Of course not! I remember vividly how my decline began. There were little gift bags that contained bite-sized candy bars. I began by eating just one candy bar out of one sack—and continued until all the sacks were empty and I had eaten my first frozen cookie! When I ate that cookie, I finally came to my senses and threw all of them away, along with the rest of the desserts.

When weigh-in day came and I had gained weight, I confessed what had been going on to my First Place 4 Health leader, and started over again. I struggled for the next three months to maintain the balance I had found that first month; however, it became harder and harder to resist temptation. Could it be that I still believe, somewhere deep down, that I can do this on my own? Instead of telling God that I am powerless and must have His help, I keep "white-knuckling" this thing called temptation and failing every time.

"If God is for us, who can be against us?" (Rom. 8:31). It saddens me to say that most of the time, the answer to that question is *me*. To blame our enemy, the devil, is pointless. The enemy brings temptation, but he doesn't have the power to make us do anything. We have been given the power of choice, and when we do wrong, it is because we have chosen to do wrong.

The devil will never tempt us to do good. First Peter 5:8 tells us to "be self-controlled and alert. Your enemy the devil prowls around like a roaring lion, looking for someone to devour." The devil wants to keep us defeated so that we are powerless to resist his evil schemes. We must learn that, without the power of Jesus Christ and the Word of God, we will never be able to resist temptation when it comes.

In all these things we are more than conquerors through him who loved us. For I am convinced that neither death nor life, neither angels nor demons, neither the present nor the future, nor any powers, neither height nor depth, nor anything else in all creation, will be able to separate us from the love of God that is in Christ Jesus our Lord (Rom. 8:37-39).

What is your greatest desire today? Is it for a healthy body, or a healthy marriage? Do you long to see your children following God? Whatever it is, I can promise you that there will be temptations on a regular basis to keep your desires from becoming a reality. But you, through the power of the Holy Spirit living in you, can say no to temptation and yes to the love of God in Jesus.

I have a good friend who has lost over 100 pounds. Recently, she has been struggling with her eating. When I asked her what was going on she said, "I'm eating crackers. Go figure!" The enemy can use just about anything—even a cracker!—to tempt us. His desire is to get us off track one more time so that we don't reach the goal.

My day of reckoning came the second weekend of January 2009 at a First Place 4 Health "Change Your Life" event in Brandon, Mississippi. A precious girl picked us up at the airport and gave each of us an adorable polka dot box filled with snacks for our hotel room. The cute little boxes contained fruit and 100-calorie bags of crackers—along with two large sugar cookies in the shape of the state of Mississippi! Vicki Heath, who doesn't have the same problem with sweets as I do, opened one of the cookies after lunch and broke off little pieces for each of us to taste. Vicki only eats sweets that are "worthy," but I on the other hand don't seem to know the difference between worthy and unworthy . . . once I get going, I don't stop.

After we had each had a taste of the cookie, Vicki folded the cellophane and put the other half of her cookie back into the box. By the time we reached our hotel, all I could think about was my two cookies inside that polka-dot box. I made myself a pot of coffee, propped up in bed with a cup o' joe and promptly ate them both. I reasoned that I was going to eat them before the weekend was over, so why not just do it and get it over with?

How could I have known that God would ask me to share my story the next day with 300 men and women? That embarrassing setback prompted me to change number four on the "my part" list from "Begin the new food plan and write on my Live It Tracker" to "Do not eat high-fat, high-sugar desserts." I cannot handle desserts. Plain and simple, I am not tempted to overeat fruits or vegetables, but when I start eating desserts, I overeat on other foods as well.

The next four weeks were wonderful. I had given up high-fat, high-sugar desserts, and I lost weight every week. I was feeling really confident . . . until February 13 rolled around. My daughter Lisa came over to help me clean house and brought six little chocolate cookies in a Valentine bag for her daddy to eat. She had seen the Paula Deen show and raved about how easy the cookies were to make.

Well, Johnny only ate one of the cookies and left the bag with the remaining five on his night stand all day. I kept thinking about those cookies, wondering what they tasted like. I honestly intended to eat only one of them . . . but after tasting just one, I ate them all.

My behavior continued the next day, Valentine's Day. We attended a party where there were desserts in abundance, and before the party was over, I had sampled several of them. And when I began eating sweets, I also started overeating other foods, continuing for the rest of the weekend.

Monday morning showed a two-pound gain on the scale . . . again.

When will I learn? Why can I not resist? The truth is that I *can* resist. Philippians 4:13 tells me that "I can do everything through Him who gives me strength." Why do I try to white-knuckle my way through temptation instead of relying on the One who gives me strength? When I begin entertaining temptation in my thought life, I am doomed to failure. God is faithful to help me *as long as I want His help*. When my desire for food is greater than my desire for Him, I get into trouble.

Do you want to overcome so that God can bless you with the deepest desires of your heart? If so, you have the power to do it. That power is found in Christ.

How do you handle temptation? Do you feel powerless to resist whatever has you enslaved? This is your year to break the chains of sin that have you bound. If temptation has you defeated, why not stop reading and get down on your knees? Cry out to God for help and tell Him that you are sorry. He will come in like a flood to cleanse you of sin and help you resist the temptation.

You and I have the power to resist temptation, but the power is in Christ, not in us. Without His help we are doomed to fail.

Let me close this chapter with a verse that has become precious to me: "I would have despaired unless I had believed that I would see the goodness of the LORD in the land of the living" (Psalm 27:13, *NASB*). The Lord wants to show you His goodness today. Do not despair. Join Him in the land of the living!

9

Man does not live on bread alone, but on every word
that comes from the mouth of God.

MATTHEW 4:4

After six months of trying to give God a year, I am realizing that I have more problems than what I eat. My attitude and my words also need a radical makeover.

One of the blessings of being married for 50 years is that Johnny and I often know what the other is thinking and what we are going to say before we say it. Yet this blessing can become a curse when our thoughts and words don't line up with what God desires for our lives.

Johnny is a walking miracle in that he is still alive after being given a prognosis in 1997 of only two years to live. This miracle has come with a price, however. Because of the many medications he takes, his short-term memory has been affected. He has no problem with long-term memory and is every bit as sharp as he has always been. But occasionally, when we are in the car after having driven for about 10 minutes, Johnny remembers that he has left his medicine, sunglasses or whatever at the house.

It happened again last Saturday when we were on our way to a party. I usually don't say anything when we have to turn around and go back home, but my body language makes my frustration abundantly clear. Last Saturday, however, I realized that Johnny cannot help his memory loss—but I can help my attitude about it. If it bothers me so much, I can remember to grab these items myself before we leave the house to help him out.

This is the second time during the last six months that God has shown me my need for His help regarding my precious husband. The first incident had to do with Johnny's cell phone. Johnny has neuropathy in his fingers and cannot feel when the "silent mode" button on the side of his phone is pressed. Time after time, I became aggravated when I couldn't reach him, until one day I decided that getting worked up about it was a useless waste of time. I made a conscious decision to change my attitude and love my husband enough not to get angry over something he can't control. Now when I can't reach him, I ask God to bless and take care of him until we can talk again. Usually, within a little while Johnny calls to check in and all is well.

These two stories demonstrate that many of the temptations we face have an effect on our relationships with God or with other people. I am finding out on my year's journey with God that He is as interested in my loving others as He is in my loving Him. Jesus said in Mark 12:31 that the second greatest commandment is to love my neighbor as I love myself.

God is teaching me that absolutely everything in this life is about relationships. First, He desires that I have the kind of relationship with Him that helps me resist temptation. Because of our relationship, I don't do or say a thing unless it comes directly from His mouth. Because of our relationship, I choose healthy foods to eat and exercise regularly to keep my body healthy. He wants to meet with me every day to give me strength, through our relationship, to face the tasks ahead.

Secondly, God desires that I have relationships with others that bring glory to Him. He wants to help me resist the temptation to become aggravated or angry at those I encounter throughout the day. (Wouldn't this make for a more stress-free life if we could master this skill?) It has occurred to me during these last six months that the people we love most are most likely to be the recipients of our aggravation and anger. I think this may be because we are confident of their love and are sure they will forgive us for our unkind words or actions. But what a terrible way to show our appreciation for their unconditional love!

So what is the solution to the problem of our attitude? I believe that I must become aware that there is a problem—and aware that the problem is mine. I can never say, "Well, that's just the way I am." After I know that I have a problem, then I must begin to pray about it, asking God for help. I ask Him to remind me of the importance of relationships *before* I shrug my shoulders, give a big sigh or act exasperated. I have found that God wants to help me, but He wants me to ask for the help He is ready and willing to give.

What relationships need help in your life? Is it the relationship with your spouse, with your kids or with someone at work? Might it be with an aging parent who needs your compassionate care? God wants to heal the mess we have made of the relationships in our lives. Once we realize there is a problem, it is time to ask for His help.

When my aging mom came to live with us in 1999, one of the hardest three-year periods of my life began. My mom had always been my hero. She could fix anything that was broken and sew anything that needed mending. When she died on January 3, 2003, my friend Kay Smith said to me, "Carole, you have lost your greatest cheerleader." Yet the closeness of my relationships with Mom only added to the stress of watching as she struggled with dementia and was confined to a wheelchair, unable to help herself in any way. There were problems finding someone to stay with her during the day while I worked. There were problems when I got home and she didn't understand what was going on around her.

Many times I was so frustrated and near tears that I would leave her room to sit in the chair where I have my quiet time. "Lord, I cannot do this job," I prayed on numerous occasions. "You know how much I love Mom, but it is breaking my heart to see her like this day after day. If You don't help me, I will never make it." Within a couple of minutes, the peace of God would come over me and I could go back into Mom's room a different person.

This kind of help is available to everyone who knows the Lord Jesus personally. The Holy Spirit of God lives inside of you and me, waiting for us to ask for His help. Why don't we do it?

Maybe we think we can solve our own problems if just given a little more time. Is this insanity or what? You know the definition of insanity, don't you? Let me tell you again, just in case you forgot: *Doing the same thing over and over and expecting different results.*

Or maybe we don't feel deserving of God's help. We secretly believe the old saying, "You've made your bed, now lie in it." Your spouse might not be the person God would have chosen for you to marry, but it is not God's will for you to live in misery for the rest of your life. He wants to heal your marriage, to make you and your spouse compatible and in love like you were at one time.

Our God specializes in situations that seem impossible. When we begin praying about the problem, we invite God to come in and help. He is only too happy to show us what our part of the problem is so that we can start doing what we must do to make it better. Then God is able to work on the other person to begin healing the relationship. The problem, many times, is that we want God to work on the other person before we begin the hard work of changing our attitude.

It has been said that "it's not what you eat, it's what's eating you." God knows that our external problems stem from internal problems of the heart. He desires to heal our hearts completely, if we will only let Him.

Remember the list you made of daily tasks, the activities that are *your* part of your year with God? These daily exercises in obedience are the starting point of a changed life. If we do our part, God is able to do His part to give us the deepest desires of our heart, including healed and whole relationships and a growing ability to resist temptation when it comes.

Here is a prayer to pray when we are tempted:

Dear Lord, I want my relationships to bring honor and
glory to You. Help me right now as I am tempted to say or
do something that dishonors You.
Help me to stop right now and adjust my attitude.
Help me to think of the ultimate consequences of my potential action.
Oh God, I want to stop my destructive behavior
and I know I cannot change my attitude without Your help.
In Jesus' name,
Amen.

10

You were running a good race.
Who cut in on you and kept you from obeying the truth?
GALATIANS 5:7

My relapses have come into sharp focus since I decided to give God a year. Each relapse is crystal clear in my mind, and my only consolation is that the time between them is becoming longer because I am so acutely aware of each one.

It pains me to tell you how many different areas of my life suffer relapse. I decide to be proactive in an area of my life, doing things when they need to get done, but then I fall back into my old ways once again. One area where I relapse has to do with my clothes. I take something off, and instead of deciding right then whether or not it needs to go to the cleaners, I put the garment on a hanger and hang it on a doorknob to deal with later. I rarely take action until I have clothes hanging on three or four doorknobs, and finally I make the decision to either take them to the cleaners or place them in the closet.

My emails are another area where I suffer relapse. It seems as though I often come to a point where I have so many emails that it's better to start from scratch. I clean out my inbox and delete every last one, and decide that I'll never let it come to that again. But before you know it, my inbox is filled to overflowing, a mess once again because I didn't stay on top of deleting or archiving as I went.

Last weekend in Dallas, I was downloading my emails to my cell phone. The phone crashed under the weight of 2,000 emails. I had to erase everything in order to use the phone while I was out of town. As a consequence, I have nothing in the memory on my cell phone—every time I need to make a call, I have to look up the number on my computer's address book.

Eating sweets, as I've mentioned, is another area where I relapse. This is an area that is particularly painful, because eating healthy foods is on my list of seven daily activities to be done in obedience to God. When I relapse and eat sweets, I'm not just neglecting to be proactive; I am being disobedient.

I could go on and on recounting all the areas of my life where I relapse into old ways and bad habits—but you get the picture. What is the common denominator of all these relapses? *Entertaining tempting thoughts.* Every relapse begins with a thought, followed by another thought, followed by another thought . . . and before we know it, we have made the wrong decision or neglected to make the right decision.

For example, if you have decided to give God a year to work on your marriage or to heal another relationship, there are certain good actions that you know you must do as your part of the equation. You might be going along just fine, but suddenly you begin to entertain the thought that you are doing good while the other person is not responding. That thought leads you to think that it's just not fair for you to do all the heavy lifting. That thought leads you to think that maybe it's not worth it, and you decide to stop doing the next right thing. Before you know it, you've dropped right back into the pit of despair.

The apostle Paul wrote about this downward spiral in Romans 7. Paul admits that he does the thing he hates and doesn't do the thing he wants to do: "I see another law at work in the members of my body, waging war against the law of my mind and making me a prisoner of the law of sin at work within my members" (Rom. 7:23). Paul was acutely aware of his own relapses into bad behavior and of his seeming inability to do the good things he desired to do.

So what is the answer to relapse? The Bible has an answer for every problem we have in this life. In 2 Corinthians 10:5, we discover that we will not be victorious over the temptation to relapse until we learn to capture our thoughts before they lead us down the wrong path: "We demolish arguments and every pretension that sets itself up against the knowledge of God, and we take captive every thought to make it obedient to Christ."

Is it possible to grab a thought before we act on it? Of course it is. The question is, do we want to?

Here's an example: When I'm at the grocery store, sometimes I see the beautiful pastries in the bakery department and think, *Johnny might like that.* Then I think, *But if I buy it, I'll eat it.* Then I either think, *Step away from the pastries!* or *It'll be fine—I'll freeze it so I don't eat it.* Once the pastry is in the basket, you can be sure that I'll eat it until it's gone.

Instead of having a drawn-out, tortured conversation with myself (that likely ends with me gobbling pastries), it's entirely possible for me to grab my first thought, say to myself, *STOP it! No pastries* and walk away. The longer I contemplate the pros and cons of buying pastries, the likelier it becomes that I will soon be eating them.

Our minds are like computers in that when the first thought comes in, we have the ability to take it to the final conclusion right then and there. Capturing our thoughts means learning a new way of thinking, contrary to the way we've always thought. I act on the first thought before the next thought takes me down the wrong path or keeps me from taking the right path.

God created us in His own image and, through the Holy Spirit, gives us the mind of Christ. We have the ability to grab our thoughts and make them subject to Christ, but we can only exercise this ability when we give up, once and for all, our right to ourselves. These bodies will never want to do the right thing, but with the mind of Christ, they can be brought under control. The way to control our bodies is to hand over our thoughts to Christ.

Will you practice taking your thoughts captive to Christ? For an entire day, write down every time you think about putting off something good that you need to do. Write down every time you think about doing something that will bring you harm. Before those thoughts lead you to entertain further thoughts, decide to act out of the mind of Christ. Stop, think and pray.

My prayers go something like this: "Lord, without Your help, I am going to eat that cookie," or "Lord, without Your help, I am going to drive too fast today. Will You help me?" When we ask for help, all the power of heaven is released on our behalf. When we don't ask for help, we are on our own.

Relapses are a part of life, but they don't have to be a permanent fixture. When we take every thought captive for Christ, we discover a way to live a life full of joy and hope—we learn the secret of controlling our thoughts.

11

And we, who with unveiled faces all reflect the Lord's glory,
are being transformed into his likeness with ever-increasing glory,
which comes from the Lord, who is the Spirit.

2 CORINTHIANS 3:18

When you give God a year to work miracles, you can expect life-changing transformation—and that includes emotional transformation. This year may not finish the healing task, but it will definitely get you started in the right direction. Those of us who have experienced pain in life—and that includes just about everyone reading this book—need healing for our emotional wounds.

Emotional pain can prompt us to act out in many ways. Some hurt people act out by being sexually promiscuous. Others use rage to squash the pain. Still others hurt their own bodies by cutting, starving themselves or eating compulsively. Since my area of ministry deals with people who deal with their pain by eating destructively, I'm going to camp on this subject for a minute.

I have said many times that losing weight is not the problem; *gaining* weight is the problem. Most of us have lost weight before, but the vast majority gain it back again. I can think of only a handful of individuals who have come into First Place 4 Health, learned how to lose their excess weight, reached their goal and then gone on with their lives without a backward glance at the scale. Many First Place 4 Health members, even after they have reached their goals, come back for a "refresher course" when their weight gain begins to reflect a life that is again out of balance.

Then there are others whom we affectionately call "lifers," who come into First Place 4 Health and never leave. Even when they reach their goal weight, they are reluctant to leave the program because they fear that they will gain all the weight back they have worked so hard to lose.

One member lost 130 pounds twice, only to gain it back each time. The last time she regained the weight, she had gastric bypass surgery, thinking that she would never be able to lose and maintain the weight loss.

In the year after surgery she lost 100 pounds, but in the years since, she has regained half of that weight.

There is no quick fix for a problem that has plagued us for years. Can you guess why? Because chronic overeating is less about food than it is about emotions.

In the rewrite of the First Place 4 Health program, we knew that we had to address the emotional component of compulsive overeating. God brought Cindy Schirle, a professional counselor, into our lives through her friend Vicki Heath, a First Place 4 Health staff member. When I heard Cindy's story, God impressed on my heart that she was the one to help us tackle this area of emotions and overeating.

We brought Cindy into Houston to film the DVD *Emotions and Eating*, which is part of our First Place 4 Health Member's Kit. Cindy also wrote the section of the *Member's Guide* that deals with mapping the relationship of emotions to food. The DVD was included in the Member's Kit to allow members to work on their emotional map in the privacy of their homes.

As a leader of a First Place 4 Health group, I was startled to discover that a majority of our members had not watched the DVD or done the emotional mapping exercise. Most of these members have been with me a couple of years. Some have had success in losing, but still struggle with the constant yo-yo effect of losing and regaining—and I just knew that the emotional aspect of overeating was an unexamined part of their struggles. Our God wants to heal the emotional area of our lives, but many of us are afraid to open the lid on all the emotions we have carefully stuffed down for so many years. I can understand how scary this must be, but I also know that until we can bring our dark secrets to the light of truth we cannot begin the healing process.

Six weeks into the second session, I made the decision to show the DVD in class, even if it meant opening a huge can of emotional worms. We watched it together for three weeks, showing a short portion each week so that we would also have time for our Bible study discussion. I asked the members to do the emotional mapping exercise and even offered prizes for those who completed it. After three weeks, most of them had finally done it. I was amazed to hear their stories, and wondered how they had survived the painful lives they have endured.

Each week, as our members shared what they were learning through the emotional mapping exercise, our love and respect for each other deepened. Shame and guilt, which had been borne for so many years, began to lift. A couple of the ladies decided to seek counseling because they realized that they have deeper wounds that need God's healing touch.

With the permission of the members of my group, I have included below several of the stories shared in our group. (Although the members are real, their names have been changed to protect their privacy.)

Susan—*I was an overweight child and my mom constantly criticized me and called me unkind names for overeating, which caused a lot of anger and shame. I realized that I am afraid to get angry because what if I am unable to stop the anger once I start? So I overeat to stuff my anger.*

Linda—*I was thin until my mom had an emotional breakdown and we kids went to live in another city with my aunt. We loved it there, but when I returned home at the age of 12, I had gained 20 pounds. The weight became a problem I lived with until I came to First Place 4 Health. I also became a compulsive shopper and continued this destructive behavior into my marriage.*

Shirley—*Ours was such a strict household that we had to finish everything on our plate or sleep at the table until the food was eaten. My mom never let me have anything sweet. Kool-Aid was sweetened with orange juice. When no one was home, I would dump out all the cereal, pick out the squares with the most sparkly sugar on them and pour the rest back into the box. I found out about the Girl Scout cookies they would buy and hide in the bottom of the freezer. I would sneak into the garage and pull out a sleeve of Thin Mints, stuff them in my pants and run outside to eat them.*

All my life I have used food to give me what I was longing for . . . love. Somehow, sugar makes me feel better. I love sugar. Through years of sexual abuse rewarded by food, I never learned that I was worth loving or how to show love without food. Anytime I have stress, sadness, am happy or experience any emotion, it seems like food just goes with it perfectly.

Pam—*I began to eat to deal with my sorrow and shame when my boyfriend broke up with me at age 26. I was devastated and felt totally rejected for the first time in my life. Many other things happened in my life, including the loss of my career as a professional musician due to a spinal cord injury. After a few years of grieving the loss of my career and incredible physical pain, I weighed 230 pounds.*

When I met Carole Lewis at an Inspire Women conference in February 2008, I was in dangerous shape physically, mentally and emotionally. At 230 pounds and 5 feet tall, I was having chest pains, stroke-level high blood pressure and depression, and I was trying to cover it all up. Carole said she could help me, and in April 2008, I began my journey toward health. Now, one year later, I have lost 35 pounds (and inches galore), and am learning to turn to the Lord and His Word for my daily emotional sustenance.

A friend once told me that dealing with emotional pain is like going to the orthodontist. The job of the orthodontist is to move bone, and that takes a long time. Patients have frequent appointments to tighten the braces that move crooked teeth into proper alignment. After about two years, the braces are removed and patients begin wearing retainers so that their teeth don't slip back into their former crooked state.

In a similar way, those who have suffered any kind of abuse or emotional trauma find that their emotions are crooked. Yes, it will take time—just like straightening crooked teeth—but total healing *is* possible with God.

"I was despised, forsaken, abused . . . and so was my Savior," says my friend and ministry associate Jan Coates. I'll let Jan tell her own story:

Shhhh, Mama's still asleep. At age five, I stood on my tip-toes and reached in the pantry for the big jar of peanut butter and bread. Being careful not to scratch the kitchen floor, I inched a chair to the counter to make a sandwich. I wanted to eat while I walked to kindergarten. I even remembered to wash the messy knife. But I was too loud.

Her feet stomped behind me. She held a belt in her fist. "Why haven't you left yet?!" She whipped my skinny legs. "Stupid, don't you know anything?" Then Mama handed me a quarter to buy candy. *Maybe she's sorry this time.*

I bought a Hershey bar and inhaled sweetness through the dark wrapper. After a nibble, I decided to save the rest for later. Something to look forward to. A patrol guard at school spotted my chocolate. She demanded that I hand it over.

Giving away my Hershey bar, I stared at the sidewalk. Peeking back, I saw the girl eat it. *Don't cry.* I clicked my pretend control button to kill my feelings.

Even before age five, evil lies had wormed holes into my soul, heart and memory:

You can't trust anybody.
Nobody loves you.
You're messy, stinky and stupid.

I added Patrol Girl to the list of people who'd hurt me. Self-hatred and bitterness settled in my heart like cement.

My school picture from second grade shows my desperation. Rather than face Mama's wrath at my knotted hair, I cut out chunks of tangles. Even today, I see terror in those seven-year-old eyes and whisper healing truth: "For I know the plans I have for you," declares the Lord, "plans to prosper you and not to harm you, plans to give you hope and a future" (Jeremiah 29:11).

Daddy tried. He took me to church and we read the Bible together, but like everybody else, he was afraid of Mama. Surely God loved good church ladies, but me? At age nine, I asked Jesus into my heart. I entered the warm baptismal water and watched my white gown float. *You can't ever be good as an angel, but this is what it feels like.*

The sparkling-clean feeling didn't last long. Almost before my hair had dried, a relative sexually molested me. I told Mama. She called me a trouble-maker and beat me with a metal clothes hanger.

Later, my mother was diagnosed with paranoid schizophrenia, manic depression, alcoholism and drug addiction. She believed everything that went wrong was my fault. So did I.

Like other abuse victims, I learned to disconnect from pain. But manifestations of physical, sexual and emotional abuse clung like leeches—hives, bedwetting, promiscuity, drugs and alcohol. My goal? To hide from myself. Escape the ugly, smelly pest named Jan.

At seventeen, married, pregnant and miserable, I added God to the snake-like list of offenders. Soon we divorced and I raised my son, Chris, alone. Years later, I remarried. Despite my college degree, name-brand clothes and nice house, I remained a broken little girl.

Three months after the wedding, a drunk driver killed Chris. My only reason to live. I died too, leaving arms and legs, a blank face without a spirit. I didn't eat, sleep, talk or glance in a mirror.

God hates me. I can't trust Him.

But out of my only son's death, the holy sledgehammer of truth begin to chip away at my dead, unforgiving heart. Miraculously over time, God resurrected me and changed my stony heart to a heart of flesh. He ministered healing through professional counselors, transparent women and the Bible.

Numbly, I'd memorized Scripture as a child. One morning pieces of Isaiah 53 returned to me like forgotten friends:

He was despised and forsaken . . .
He was pierced for our transgressions . . .
He was oppressed and afflicted . . .
Like a lamb led to slaughter . . .
By His stripes we are healed . . .

"Jesus, oh sweet Jesus. You understand. *You* were abused. God, Your only Son died, too." Kneeling in the den, I began to forgive those who'd hurt me—everybody from Patrol Girl to the drunk driver who killed Chris. Palms open and high, I released rage and cried, "I need You."

Women everywhere, in malls, in grocery stores and at PTA meetings, appeared almost spotlighted. *See her eyes? She needs My love. Those long sleeves hide bruises. That prostitute by the stop sign? She's a child-abuse victim. Smell the alcohol on your friend's breath? She's trying to escape. See the woman in the buffet line? She's trying to smother her pain. Show them your scars.*

Compelled by my ongoing healing, I wrote *Set Free: God's Healing Power for Abuse Survivors and Those Who Love Them.* The book reveals the pain of six women. A part of me, of every abused child, lies in each one.

Meet Elaine, the daughter of evil; Liz, the keeper of shameful secrets; Debi, the prostitute; Gayle, the daughter of condemnation; Karissa, the party girl; and Gloria, the hardened heart. You might discover yourself or someone you know.

The child abuse statistics are harrowing:

- Every two minutes a child is sexually assaulted.
- Fifty million women in the U.S., or one in three, were abused as children.
- Two children die daily in the U.S. at the hands of an abuser.
- Eighty percent of substance abusers were abused as children.

- Ninety-five percent of prostitutes were victims of child abuse.
- Abused victims often marry abusers.
- Up to 80 percent of obese women endured childhood maltreatment.

For those who survive, the damage includes brain injuries leading to changes in memory, emotion and basic drives; STDs; mental retardation; speech problems; depression; low self-esteem; self-destructiveness; physical aggression and adolescent pregnancy.

We have an Advocate who understands. He's been there, too. Despite the rawness of abuse, there's healing and forgiveness bought through bloody redemption of our Savior.[1]

One of Jan's favorite promises from Scripture is "I am the LORD, who heals you" (Exod. 15:26). She has held on to that promise for decades, knowing that what the Bible says is truth—not just for the "perfect" Christian lady, but for every human, regardless of his or her past. That means you, me and the rest of the world.

That's reassuring, isn't it? As Jan's testimony attests, healing from the trauma of childhood abuse *is a process*. It's a journey that requires accepting God's love right where you are, support from your First Place 4 Health small group, prayer, journaling and faith in God.

This process is part of the journey toward total balance in all areas of our life. Healing from the inside out, including wounds from childhood trauma and abuse, is a process. If you're ready to:

- feel worthy to call on God;
- have a peaceful heart;
- be set free from your past;
- experience healing and wholeness;
- claim God's promises to give you hope and a bright future;
- submit your life to Jesus and start today as a new beginning;

then know that God can and will help you make these changes in your life. It's your decision to say, "Yes, Lord, I want freedom. I want to live from this day forward with good physical and mental health, emotional well-being and a personal, loving relationship with You."

For some, Christian counseling is an excellent place to learn coping skills and face painful truth in a safe environment. Many healing overcomers begin their journey in the presence of God, knowing that God's Word sets the captives free. Scripture is designed to comfort you, to help you know God and to help you claim God's promises. I encourage you to read, memorize and treasure in your heart the verses below:

On Fear

- **Psalm 34:4:** "I sought the Lord, and he answered me; he delivered me from all my fears."
- **Isaiah 41:13:** "For I am the Lord, your God, who takes hold of your right hand and says to you, Do not fear; I will help you."
- **Romans 8:15:** "For you did not receive a spirit that makes you a slave again to fear, but you received the Spirit of sonship. And by him we cry, 'Abba, Father.'"
- **1 John 4:18:** "There is no fear in love. But perfect love drives out fear, because fear has to do with punishment. The one who fears is not made perfect in love."

On Anger

- **Proverbs 15:1:** "A gentle answer turns away wrath, but a harsh word stirs up anger."
- **Proverbs 29:8:** "Mockers stir up a city, but wise men turn away anger."
- **Ecclesiastes 7:9:** "Do not be quickly provoked in your spirit, for anger resides in the lap of fools."
- **Ephesians 4:31:** "Get rid of all bitterness, rage and anger, brawling and slander, along with every form of malice."

On Hope

- **Psalm 31:24:** "Be strong and take heart, all you who hope in the LORD."
- **Psalm 42:5:** "Why are you downcast, O my soul? Why so disturbed within me? Put your hope in God, for I will yet praise him, my Savior and my God."
- **Psalm 71:14:** "But as for me, I will always have hope; I will praise you more and more."
- **Romans 5:5:** "And hope does not disappoint us, because God has poured out his love into our hearts by the Holy Spirit, whom he has given us."

Beth Moore, a friend and well-known Christian author and speaker, says that her healing from sexual abuse was like peeling the skin off an onion. Layer after layer of pain had to come off before she got to the real person underneath. Beth's book *Breaking Free* is a great resource for anyone who is in the process of healing from abuse. Her healing demonstrates the healing power found in God's Word, through prayer and by fully giving your life to the One who heals and sets us free.

Interestingly, neither Beth nor Jan have ever had problems with weight. Both ladies suffered deep pain and trauma, but chose healthy diets and regular exercise as tools to cope, rather than letting food be their false comforter.

A large number of both men and women who struggle with addictions, such as food, drugs, alcohol, tobacco or sex, in their adult lives, endured some form of mistreatment during their childhoods. It is time for the Body of Christ to claim God's promises of freedom and help each other to be set free.

Your eating may be out of control because you are in a difficult marriage and you don't have any hope that it will ever be better. I'm sure you have found that overeating only makes the problem worse. Many women have told me, "My husband should love me unconditionally whether I'm fat or thin." That may be true, but your emotional wellbeing has nothing to do with your mate's acceptance—it has everything to do with God's unconditional love. Your difficult marriage may be the "heavenly sandpaper" the Lord Jesus is using to draw you into a closer relationship with Him. Years ago, Evelyn Christiansen wrote a wonderful book called *Lord, Change Me.* In it, she wrote that when we ask God to change us instead of the "difficult" person, He shows us our own sin. Then, as we begin to change, we see others around us change too.

Jesus spoke to this truth in Luke 6:41-42:

> Why do you look at the speck of sawdust in your brother's eye and pay no attention to the plank in your own eye? How can you say to your brother, "Brother, let me take the speck out of your eye," when you yourself fail to see the plank in your own eye? You hypocrite, first take the plank out of your eye, and then you will see clearly to remove the speck from your brother's eye.

The emotional area of our lives has a profound effect on our relationships: relationships with our spouse, with our children, with co-workers and with others we encounter every day. When our emotional lives are damaged, we have a tendency to likewise damage our relationships. And if we refuse to recognize that we need healing in our hearts, our relationships are not likely to change for the better.

Giving God a year is the perfect time to begin the hard work of emotional healing and relationship building. Won't you ask God to show you your untended, unhealed emotional wounds? Don't be afraid. He is the Lord who heals you.

"Doctors, nurses, family members, and well-meaning pastors had written Mom off as hopeless," says Jan Coates. Her story goes on:

> Mental institutions, tranquilizers and shock treatments, coupled with drug and alcohol abuse, made her life a living hell and hurt all of us, even though we tried to understand that she was hopelessly trapped by her illness and addictions.

Mom's worsened condition destroyed our family. After twenty-five years of marriage, Dad divorced Mom and gave her a generous cash settlement that could have provided for her for at least twenty years. She spent the entire sum in less than twelve months. My siblings and I felt forced to support her and find her a suitable apartment.

One snowy night, my boss, Mike, was with me as I drove out of a parking garage. "Hey, Jan," he teased. "Ten points if you can hit the bag lady."

Three feet away was a woman bundled in a tattered coat, wearing two brightly colored hats with a scarf draped around her neck and face. Mismatched mittens protected her hands, and she carried two overstuffed black trash bags. When she turned and stared at me with her piercing blue eyes, I died inside. She didn't recognize me, but I certainly knew her.

Cursing silently, I said, *Oh, God! Don't let her see me. Don't let Mike know that bag lady is my mother.*

I laughed at Mike's joke and pressed the accelerator, veering around and past the woman in the tattered coat. I didn't want a second look at her, but guilt consumed me. *She's your mother*, my conscience said. *She may be crazy, but she needs help.*

I dropped Mike off at the office, drove a few blocks, and stopped the car. I couldn't see to drive—the tears flowed too heavily. I screamed at her. I beat my fists against the steering wheel. Memories of the past flowed through my mind. "God, why can't You help her?" I screamed.

After my chest quit heaving and my screams silenced, I realized that I couldn't keep her from roaming the streets during a blizzard, but at least I could help her stay warm and fed. I drove to a farm supply store and bought her a pair of insulated black boots and a pair of waterproof ski gloves. Then, at a corner grocery store, I purchased bread, crackers, canned chicken, soup, milk, eggs, sliced cold cuts and cheese.

Weeks earlier, I had placed her in a government-subsidized apartment. I went there, and her name was still on the mailbox. Anticipating her violent reaction, I trembled as I knocked on the brown metal door. "It's your daughter. Open up."

Mom opened the door, wearing a toothless grin and her latest "Goodwill special" outfit: stained dark blue slacks and a man's plaid shirt. "Come in, sweetie," she said. Her voice was soft, a tone I rarely heard before. "I hoped you would visit me."

Holding back tears, I looked around her small three-room home. All the clothing and toiletries I had purchased for her over the years were stuffed in trash bags and stacked on the floor of her living room. She had stale food and junk from the dumpsters stored in other trash bags.

"I brought you some goodies," I said, tearing my gaze from the bags. "You may have to move the beer out of the refrigerator to make room for food."

"No beer, Jan. I'm not allowed to drink anymore. It's bad for me."

"No beer? Really?'"

She nodded. "I threw out all the drugs, too. They were making me sick."

Hundreds of times in the past she had told me she was through with drugs and beer. And she was—for a few hours.

Don't let her get to you. Put up the iron front. "It's okay, Mom. You're over sixty years old, and I'm a grown woman. You don't have to tell me stories."

"I'm not telling you stories," she said. "I have a job. I go to work. I go to Bible study. I got baptized and accepted Jesus as my Savior. This summer I'm going to camp. Come with me tonight for dinner. You'll see."

I had heard crazy things from my mother before, but this was the craziest yet. I stared at her for several seconds before I decided to call her bluff. "Okay, what time?"

"We need to leave now," she said. "We have to hurry."

We got into the car and drove the dark, snowy downtown streets until we arrived outside a weathered building. The sign on the outside read "The Salvation Army."

"I can't wait for all my friends to meet you," she said. "I'm proud of you. You're my daughter." She looped her arm through mine and escorted me into the building.

What is going on here? This was the sanest, calmest conversation I'd had with my mother since I was a child.

Several people stood in the food line with their plastic trays. One dropped out of line to help Mom find a seat. Another brought her a plate piled high with food. They warmly hugged Mom, and she hugged them.

My mother hugs people?

One of the Army's officers sat beside Mom and another across from her. They spoke softly to her and seemed to genuinely care about her. Mom smiled more during the next half hour than I had observed during my entire childhood.

Someone brought me a tray and made a place for me next to Mom, but my stomach was in knots and I couldn't eat. Throughout dinner, Mom hummed "When the Saints Go Marching In." She smiled frequently and laughed several times.

No one said anything when she stuffed her leftover food into the ever-present trash bag.

These people liked my mother—they really liked her. I could hardly take in what was going on in front of me. Several more people hugged her, called her by name, and treated her like a normal human being.

Slowly I began to understand that a transformation had taken place in her life. God had done what dozens of doctors couldn't do: He healed a broken, mentally ill woman with unconditional love, shining through others. For the first time in my life, I saw peace and love in my mother's heart—a peace beyond description and a tender love that I'd always hoped we'd share.

At the table, Mom leaned against me, wrapped her right arm around my shoulder, and pulled me tight. With her left hand, she snatched the dinner rolls off my plate. I laughed and grinned at her. She still had some crazy traits left.

She smiled and said, "I love you."

My grin vanished and tears ran down my cheeks. I couldn't speak for several minutes. Mom and I had finally connected at the heart level. I turned from my uneaten food and stared deeply into Mom's eyes and then at her Salvation Army friends. What I couldn't say to those friends then but say only later was this: "When I could no longer love her, you embraced her. Through your love, God answered my spoken and unspoken prayers and set Mom free from her addictions. You loved her and showered her with God's love, right where she was—craziness and all. Because of you, I found a mother—a real mother. I had given up hope, but the Lord never did."

I hope you are as blessed as I have been by Jan's testimony. There's always a rainbow after the storms, as Jan's story boldly affirms.

Sometimes it takes an army to heal the broken from the inside out. Through the Salvation Army, Jan's mother rededicated her life to Jesus Christ and lived the last 10 years of her life with a peace that passes all understanding. Today, Jan knows for certain that her mother is in heaven.

Hope? God never gives up. The new you—filled to the brim with balanced and healthy emotions, mind, body and spirit—is a miracle waiting to happen through the power of Jesus Christ.

Note

1. Jan Coates is the author of *Set Free: God's Healing Power for Abuse Survivors and Those Who Love Them*, which I wholeheartedly recommend, and founder of Set Free Today (www.setfreetoday.com), a ministry where you can come as you are and leave with a new beginning. Jan is an author, speaker and encourager. She is a frequent conference speaker and appears on national television and radio programs. For additional information, please email her at jan@jancoates.com.

12

Therefore, since we are surrounded by such a great cloud of witnesses,
let us throw off everything that hinders and the sin that so easily entangles,
and let us run with perseverance the race marked out for us.

HEBREWS 12:1

From our first breath until our last, we are all running in a race called Life. Some finish their race in infancy, while others run their race for over 100 years. In God's economy, the length of the race is not the important part. What is important to God is *how* we run the race. If you are reading these words, you are still in the race.

Some of us started the race with obvious handicaps. They might be physical handicaps, such as cerebral palsy. Or we might have begun our race in an abusive family setting. We might have gotten a good start in the race, but then made some poor choices along the way. Perhaps you find yourself bogged down in a loveless marriage or in dire financial straits and you are only halfway to the finish line.

I believe that the most beautiful thing about being a Christian is that the day we ask Jesus Christ into our lives, the playing field at once becomes level. When we become followers of Jesus Christ, the Holy Spirit comes to live inside us and He teaches us how to run the race to win—no matter how poorly we were running before He came in.

How are you running your race? Are you running strong because you have trained adequately, or are you limping through the race called life, wishing you had not entered it at all? Training is mandatory if we are going to run strong and win. Let's look more closely at the verse above and learn how to run our own race.

We are surrounded by a great cloud of witnesses. It is a great comfort to me to know that others who have finished their race are now in heaven cheering me on toward the finish line. I have my dad and mother and daughter Shari in my cheering section. I have great Christian friends in heaven who are cheering me on, as well. The saints listed in Hebrews 11 are in my cheering section rooting for me. But better than all of these is the fact that the

Lord Jesus is sitting at the right hand of God, talking to the Father about me (and about you!). I can imagine Jesus saying to the Father, "Look at my sister Carole. I know she has what it takes inside of her to finish strong. She's down there praying right now, asking for help because she knows We will help her today. Father, I know she doesn't look like a marathon runner, but with Our help, she will win this race."

When I competed in a half-marathon in January 2006, I am sorry to say that I didn't train well for the race. That year was the twenty-fifth anniversary of the First Place 4 Health program, and we invited participants in the program to join us in Houston for the race. It was wonderful seeing all those who signed up to join us. There was Cheri, who signed up for the 5K (three mile) walk, who has severe cerebral palsy and walks with the help of a walker. There was Melody, who is legally blind. Melody went into training and signed up for the 5K walk as well. Mark, who has lost over 100 pounds in our program, trained for a year to run the full marathon. That year, Mark signed up for three 5K races, three 10K races, three half-marathons and three marathons. He finished all 12 races.

We had a dinner of spaghetti at the church the night before, and were all excited when we began the race the next morning. As the sun came up over the George Brown Convention Center in downtown Houston, we began to walk and run. Runners had flown in from all over the world to compete that day, and the next morning in the paper their names were listed as the winners—but the truth is that we were *all* winners, because we all finished the race. Our team of 20 First Place 4 Health competitors might not have looked like some of the world-class runners, but we were there that day to run our own personal best—and to finish. That is exactly what happened.

I had two friends with me the entire 13.1 miles, but even with their company and encouragement, the race was harder than I expected because I had not trained for it; I walk and jog three miles on the treadmill each morning, but three miles is a little different than 13.1 miles. We had a great time covering the course through our great city. We walked most of the time, but when we saw a mile marker coming up, we started running in case there was a TV camera! I had my cell phone with me, and I called Johnny at home throughout the race to tell him where I was at the time.

My goal was to finish under four hours so that I could have my picture taken before they took the clock down. When the three of us crossed the finish line 3 hours and 45 minutes after we began, it didn't matter one bit that others had finished the entire marathon—twice the distance—in less time. What mattered were the people on both sides of the track cheering like crazy for us to cross the finish line.

This is the picture in my mind's eye of the life-race you and I are running. The great cloud of witnesses in heaven—those who have finished their race to God's glory—has become our cheering section, waiting at the finish line to embrace us.

Throw off everything that hinders. What is hindering you from running your race? There were thousands of First Place 4 Health members and leaders who did not choose to sign up for the Houston Marathon, but there were 20 who did. It seems that a prerequisite for running is signing up to run. When you asked Jesus into your life, that was the day you signed up.

I'm sure there were many who signed up and paid their registration money to run the Houston Marathon who didn't show up the day of the race. There were probably many reasons they didn't show up that morning, ranging from personal illness to having a fight with their spouse or child to just plain not feeling like running. Signing up is not enough to get us in the race; only showing up will get the job done. Remember what I've said before: "Eighty percent of life is just showing up." To "throw off everything that hinders" means making a decision after we sign up to show up every day for training.

In the Christian life, our training looks something like this:

- Having a daily time of prayer, Bible study and Scripture memory
- Eating healthy foods to keep our bodies strong
- Exercising on a regular basis to build our strength
- Getting adequate rest each night
- Managing stress on a daily basis
- Actively working on loving relationships with those we love and with those we don't
- Receiving healing from God of emotional pain

What is hindering you today, keeping you from showing up for the race? Is it your physical body, which is in such poor condition that you don't feel up to running? Is it something emotional, such as depression over a seemingly hopeless situation in your life? Is it a mental hindrance, the thought that you just don't want to do the hard work to show up every day to train? Or could it be that spiritually you are in a wrestling match with God, your trainer in the race?

I'm sad to say that the last one has been my biggest hindrance during this year I said I'd give to God. The reasons or excuses are numerous. Three weeks into the race, Hurricane Ike destroyed our home and took everything we owned in one fell swoop. We have been displaced and are now living in our third home since September 2008.

Hurricane Ike definitely qualifies as a hindrance to running my year-long race with God, but the greatest hindrance I face every day is *me*. During the last seven months since the hurricane, I have struggled with God over whether or not I will be obedient to do my part so that He is free to do His part in helping me finish strong in this year-long race. I started the race strong and ran hard for three weeks before the storm hit. Since that time, it's been an uphill climb most of the time.

God has been gracious and faithful every step of the way. The three temporary homes He has provided have been wonderful and completely furnished. We have literally not needed a thing during this year. Our insurance has finally been settled, our old home has been torn down and life is moving forward. The problem lies with me; instead of doing my part—which entails refraining from desserts—I keep "feeding" my emotions with sweets. I know in my spirit that it is showdown time between me and God. Who will be the trainer and who will show up to run the race? Never has it been clearer to me that God is serious about this business of running my life's race with purpose and passion.

Here is what has happened as I have stumbled and fallen during the last year:

Physically

I'll be going along great with my eating and exercise, losing weight each week and feeling really good about the race. Then something happens, such as a problem at work or with the insurance company handling our Hurricane Ike claim, that upsets or frustrates me. The next time I'm at the grocery store, I think that maybe something sweet will make me feel better. At that moment, it doesn't matter at all that I told God I would run this race with Him for the next year. When I purchase and eat whatever it is that is my personal hindrance, I say in essence, "God, I'll take over the training now."

Before Hurricane Ike, I jumped back and forth between obedience and disobedience, but a very strange thing has happened: I believe that God has great things in store for the First Place 4 Health program, and I have become aware He wants to use me in His plans. In order for His plans for First Place 4 Health to be fulfilled, I must allow Him to be my personal trainer and end up at the finish line in victory. Since the hurricane, I have found that when I digress from the plan physically, all the others areas of my life start spiraling down as well.

I am happy to have lost six pounds during the last 12 months, but I am still not where I need to be. I plan to give God this next year, and I'm confident that He will help me reach my goal weight and stay there.

Mentally

When I go back on my pledge to give up desserts, I am unable to focus on writing this book. I set my alarm and get up early to write, but nothing happens when I sit down in front of the computer. Everything is inside my mind to write the book God wants me to write, but my own disobedience stands in the way of getting the job done. Is this a hindrance? You bet it is! My deadline for the manuscript came and went last week, and without God's help this book will not be finished.

Emotionally

When I'm disobedient in my eating and can't focus mentally to write, I start going down emotionally. For me, this emotional plunge looks like lying around doing Sudoku puzzles instead of everything else. I'm not the type to get down on myself or beat myself up emotionally; instead, I just "check out" and do something I enjoy instead of getting back on track.

Spiritually

On Monday of this week, when I weighed in, I was brought up short with the realization that the year I said I would give to God is nearly over. Am I going to obey or not? Am I going to be the runner and allow God to be my trainer? Am I going to show up every day so that He will get glory from the race I run?

When I am disobedient in my eating (physical), I can't focus to write (mental), which leads me to malaise (emotional), which ultimately leads to a decline in the spiritual area of my life as well. I begin to neglect my time with God because I know that I am not doing my part on our team. If I refuse to stay in training and show up every day, then I hinder the work of God in my life. I am the runner and God is the trainer. God wants to answer the deepest desires of my heart and help me finish the race in strength and power.

When I weighed in on Monday, I was able to tell God one more time that He needs to be the trainer and I need to be trained. I apologized for giving in one more time to the hindrances I face, and I asked again for His help. God immediately joined me back on the training field and has been there 24/7 for the last four days.

Have my circumstances changed? Not one bit. I am still living through a time of stress and struggle in the wake of Hurricane Ike. What has happened instead is that I have thrown off the hindrances that so easily entangle, and now God is able to pick me up, dust me off and put me back on track.

Precious reader, God is teaching me that this race is not about me at all. I run the race so that my life might bring glory to God. When I do, others who don't know Jesus will look at my life and want Him to be their trainer as well.

Sin that so easily entangles. Throwing off what hinders me from running my race simply means that I decide to stop sinning. Disobedience is sin. God tells me over and over in His Word that if I love Him, I will obey Him. John 14:23 says, "If anyone loves me, he will obey my teaching. My Father will love him, and we will come to him and make our home with him." Romans 6:16 says, "Don't you know that when you offer yourselves to someone to obey him as slaves, you are slaves to the one whom you obey—whether you are slaves to sin, which leads to death, or to obedience, which leads to righteousness?" God's Word is clear: We obey what we love.

Disobedience gets my life all tangled up and before I know it, I feel hopeless and don't want to show up to train. Sin is anything that keeps me from missing the mark of what God has planned for my life. He tells me in Jeremiah 29:11 that all His plans for me are good and are to prosper me and not harm me. When I choose my own way over God's way, I stop training for this race I signed up to run.

Run with perseverance. James 1:2-4 tells me:

Consider it pure joy . . . whenever you face trials of many kinds, because you know that the testing of your faith develops perseverance. Perseverance must finish its work so that you may be mature and complete, not lacking anything.

Running with perseverance simply means that if I do my part by signing up and showing up to train for this race, God will do His part to help me win it. Yes, I've relapsed on my commitment to give God a year, and you probably will, too. But it is never too late to start training again. The race is God's, and if I allow Him to be my trainer, He will indwell this flawed body and empower me to finish this year-long marathon victorious. Trials and tribulations—that is, hindrances—are important to our spiritual growth because they help us learn how to persevere and stay in the race to the end. If you have fallen down, get back up right now, throw off the sin that entangles you and go back into training with God. Finish the race you signed up for. God will enable you to persevere through the trials that seem to stand in your way.

The race marked out for us. This last part of the verse is my favorite phrase from Hebrews 12:1. Each of us needs to thank God that He has called us to run our own race. I am not called to run your race, and you are not called to run mine. God has a race marked out that is perfectly designed for you, which will conform you to the image of His Son, Jesus, as you run it (see Rom. 8:29). As each of us runs the race that God has set out for us, we will learn how to throw off whatever hindrances we have in our life. We will learn how to be obedient and to quit sinning willfully, and in the process we will begin to look like Jesus.

You might be thinking that God has given you the worst possible course to run. I believe that God knows us so well and loves us so perfectly that the race we find marked out for us is perfectly suited to make us look more like Jesus. Life's trials and tribulations are God's heavenly sandpaper designed to smooth those rough places that don't resemble Jesus.

These are the questions before us: Will we sign up for the race? Will we show up to train for the race? Will we run the race? Will we finish the race?

Get back in the race! I'll run with you and cheer you on as we go. And here's even better news: God will run every step of the race with us, and will be there when we cross the finish line.

APPENDIX A

CAROLE'S GIVE GOD A YEAR JOURNAL

Week 1

August 25–August 31, 2008

We were anticipating the landfall of Hurricane Gustav somewhere between New Orleans and Galveston. When the Category 1 hurricane made landfall, New Orleans and our nation was spared catastrophic damage.

Our kids came to the Bay over the weekend to help us load Johnny's cargo trailer. We are going to store it away from our home on high ground until hurricane season is over the end of November. Lisa and Lisa [my daughter and daughter-in-law] were helping me inside while John and Kent [my son and son-in-law] were helping Johnny in the garage. We were going to load all of my mom's boxes into the trailer when the girls said, "Let's not do this again. Let's go through the boxes and dispose of this stuff once and for all." We worked from 8:00 A.M. until midnight, only stopping for meals. Praise God, we finished the task that I have thought about and worried about since 1999! The girls took all the pictures of their families and whatever items they wanted. We made a big box for the Symank girls [my daughter Shari's children] and had three big garbage cans of throwaways. When we finished, the closets were all clean and ready to use for other things. I felt like a thousand pounds had been lifted off my shoulders after this monumental task was completed.

I wrote the Introduction and first two chapters of a new book, *Give God a Year*. I talked with Bill Greig, President of Gospel Light, about the book being published and coming out by the end of 2009.

We looked at seven possible office spaces for the move to new offices, getting ready for the change from being a ministry of Houston's First Baptist Church to a non-profit 501(c)3 corporation.

I received so many answers to prayer this week—Cara and Luke, no hurricane, and Mom's things disposed of after almost 10 years of moving the boxes around. Great meetings, got so much work done, Johnny felt good all week.

Completed all seven items on my list every day! Yeah!

Lost 5 pounds!!!!!

Week 2

September 1–7, 2008

Wrote two more chapters for *Give God a Year*. Wrote Annotated Table of Contents for Kim Bangs. Wrote new Introduction for 2009 Prayer Journal.

Completed all seven items on my list every day!

Saturday I hand washed my car and bathed the dog. Bought groceries, colored my hair, watered the flowers. Ate healthy all day.

Got up before 3:00 A.M. three days this week to write and haven't experienced fatigue one minute. This is a miracle, as I normally need 7 to 8 hours of sleep a night. God is doing something here and multiplying my sleep in the process.

Got up at 2:30 A.M. Sunday to write and prepare to worship in our brand-new sanctuary today. I am meeting two persons who haven't attended church in a while.

Proposal for First Place 4 Health to become 501(c)3 unanimously approved by Deacon Administrative Committee.

Week 3

September 8–14, 2008

The week started out well and I finished chapter 6 on the new book. On Wednesday, we received word that Hurricane Ike was heading for Galveston, so we began the process of packing up to leave. John and Lisa came on Wednesday to help us pack; they moved all our plants and lawn furniture into the garage and took the boat back to Houston when they left. Our friends Nick and Euphanel Goad called on Thursday morning and left word for us to evacuate to their retreat center at Round Top. I called Euphanel to see if our pets could come and she said, "Bring them, too." We were able to get Archie, one of our two cats, into a carrier but the other one, Yellow Cat, shot out the door, so he stayed at the Bay because we were unable to coax him back into the house.

On Friday night, Hurricane Ike came into Galveston and its path came right over our home. Early Saturday morning, our next door neighbors, Greg and Melissa Jones, drove down to the Bay. They had to walk over two miles because the roads were flooded, but they were able to take pictures of the area as they walked. They both knew what they were going to find before they ever got to our house, because every home they saw that was ground-level was gutted by the storm surge. Melissa and Greg's home was fine, because it was new and built on pilings. The downstairs was destroyed, but they didn't even have a picture crooked on the wall upstairs. Melissa called me from San Leon and she was sobbing so hard I could barely understand her. She told me that our home was destroyed and there wasn't even any furniture inside. I asked her to take pictures so we could see what had happened and she said, "Are you sure you want pictures?"

That night, Greg and Melissa drove to Round Top Retreat to personally show us the pictures. Greg said, "There was no way I was going to email these to you." They spent the night with us, along with our family who had traveled to Round Top so we could all be together.

Week 4

September 15–21, 2008

On Monday, we drove to the Bay to retrieve whatever we could. I had been collecting pottery of a type we received as wedding gifts in 1959, buying up pieces on eBay, and an entire upper cabinet in the kitchen was still intact and full of the pottery. All of the large pieces of pottery that were on the top of the refrigerator in the apartment were gone. Our house and all the houses around us looked the same: completely gutted by the storm surge from Hurricane Ike. Our entire fence that surrounded our property was gone. The pier was destroyed and the large deck over our boat lift was in the neighbor's yard behind our home. We found half of the headboard to our bed and parts of a few pieces of furniture, but for the most part, everything had washed out into Galveston Bay.

We found Yellow Cat on the rafters in the garage, but were unable to coax him down. On Wednesday, we went back to the Bay with a can of tuna and the cat carrier. We were able to retrieve Yellow Cat and take him back to Round Top. At least now we have all of our family together! Our daughter Lisa and her husband, Kent, came up because they had no electricity, so now we had a cook! Thank You, Lord.

It is now obvious that life as we knew it is never going to be quite the same.

Week 5

September 22–28, 2008

On Monday, we drove back to the Bay (two hour drive each way) to meet with the flood insurance adjuster. He said that our damage was definitely flood damage. There had been a storm surge that left water marks at four feet on our walls. There were holes in every room of our house. We learned this week that the only insurance that pays is the one that covers whatever did the damage. Homeowner insurance covers theft and fire. Windstorm insurance covers wind damage (and our roof didn't have one shingle missing). When the windstorm adjuster came and said he wouldn't be able to help us, we asked him about the fence being gone and he said, "We can't be sure that the wind got it; it might have been the flood." The flood insurance doesn't cover the fence, so we are in for a long road to recovery with only the flood insurance willing to pay for the destruction.

Our neighbor Allen found one of my prayer journals. It was ruined, but I was so grateful to have it. All of my prayer journals since 1990 were on top of my chest of drawers in my closet, and I would often refer back to them when I write, just to check my dates and facts for accuracy. It is curious that these types of personal items are a much greater loss than the furniture and clothes. I'm so grateful the girls took all the family pictures before the storm.

October 2008

We are still at Round Top, and Lisa is helping me construct a list of every item that was in our home. We did have a notebook with pictures of all the furniture, but trying to remember what was in every cabinet, closet and drawer is a colossal task. Lisa started an Excel spreadsheet for each room so we can add items as we remember them. I am so thankful for the Internet because we can find the value of almost anything there.

Lisa and I have enjoyed going to the Antique Festival in Round Top and the surrounding towns; however, I can't buy anything because I don't have a home to put it in.

The weather is absolutely beautiful and we are so grateful to have this wonderful place to stay. The Goads have given us an entire house to stay in and we have enough room for our family to come and go as they can.

We had our annual First Place 4 Health Wellness Week here at the Round Top Retreat this month. It worked out great because I was able to be with the group and still take care of Johnny and the pets in our home here on the grounds.

After Wellness Week was over, we moved back to the Bay into our neighbor's, Greg and Melissa's, home. It is now October 15, and we are amazed at how fast the last five weeks have flown by since Hurricane Ike.

It is much harder to be here than being at Round Top and driving back and forth; now we are living here and have to look next door at our home that is just a shell. I walk over there every day just to see if I can find something, anything of value, but that just doesn't happen.

I was obsessed with replacing our cedar fence, so we went in with Greg and Melissa and got the fence replaced. I had to laugh later because we were living up high and still could see all the devastation outside the fence. The new fence looks ridiculous amid the mess that is everywhere. Maybe we don't need to make any more decisions for a while!

The rest of the month was spent meeting with FEMA and talking with the adjusters. We can tell that nothing is going to happen fast.

November 2008

The weather is bad and we have the blues. Johnny is extremely weak and hardly leaves the bedroom at all. We have only made one purchase since Ike and that is a large flat-screen television for Johnny. He has been watching all the presidential election news.

I am doing all the grocery shopping and am very unhappy with the 21 stairs to climb when I drive up with 12 bags of groceries. I always debate whether to load up like a packhorse and try to get all the bags up in one trip or make two trips like a sane person.

I am back at work in Houston and it isn't nearly as much fun making the drive when there is no house or pier waiting for me.

We had Thanksgiving at Jeff and Kathryn's home (Shari's husband and new wife), and all the family were together, so that was very nice.

December 2008

Well, the last three months have been a whirlwind of activity, meeting with adjusters and constructing our list of everything we lost in Hurricane Ike. I haven't written one word on the book since Hurricane Ike landed September 13. Instead of a July 2009 publishing date, we are looking at a December 2009 release date. That is, if I start writing again.

I didn't put up a Christmas tree because ours was lost in the storm and I don't want to move a large Christmas tree box when we move again. Being homeless makes you think about what you want to move, so I can see why homeless people carry all their worldly possessions in a shopping cart or on their backs. I get a mental picture of us, if we were homeless, walking Meathead on a leash, with two cat carriers and a bird cage in a big wagon dragging along behind us. My sense of humor is a little jaded right now; I think the magnitude of our loss is settling in after three months of dealing with it.

The first of December, Johnny said that he thinks we need to move back to Houston, at least for the winter. I called my friend Linda, and she agreed to rent her townhome to us. On December 15, we moved back to Houston to a fully furnished place to live. God has been so good to us, and within a week of being back in Houston, Johnny's strength began returning. I believe he was depressed, but we never thought that was the problem during the two months we lived back at the Bay. Since Johnny has cancer, we always think everything stems from the cancer, but that is just not true.

We are now just 10 minutes from work and all our family. This is really nice and makes the loss much easier to handle, not having to see it every day. We had our home torn down before we moved and I thought I would feel better when it was gone, but actually it is worse.

Thank You, God, that nothing can ever take away the wonderful memories of our 11 years living on the water.

We spent Christmas Eve and Christmas Day at Lisa and Kent's home with all the family.

January 2009

January was a busy month. My birthday was January 2, and I spent the first two weeks celebrating with wonderful friends who were so glad to see me and wanted to take me out to lunch.

We had two First Place 4 Health Change Your Life events in January, one in Brandon, Mississippi, and one in Shreveport, Louisiana. It was great seeing so many who have been praying for Johnny and me since the storm. Their love is such an encouragement to my heart.

January 18–23, we hosted a SPA Week for Authors and Speakers at Round Top Retreat, which was a huge upper for me. These 21 ladies were awesome and so appreciated everything we did for them. I am anticipating great things from their lives as they give God the next year.

We are going to have an online First Place 4 Health class when they return home.

We began our new session of First Place 4 Health at the church, and I always love leading my class on Tuesday at noon.

I had a great month of eating right and exercising.

February 2009

This was a busy month, like January. Johnny and I went to his oncologist in Los Angeles the first week of February and then on to Ventura to meet with the folks at Gospel Light.

I volunteered to work on the committee planning my fiftieth high-school reunion and met one evening with all my old school friends.

On Valentine's Day, Johnny and I went to an annual luncheon of all the couples we went to church with when our kids were young. It is amazing that these 25 couples are still together and that their children are all doing well. Could it be the positive influence of raising your children in a Christian home?

I loved speaking at Celebrate Recovery this month. Anyone struggling with any kind of addiction relates to others who are struggling as well. What a great ministry.

We had another Change Your Life event in Kernersville, North Carolina, this month, and I so love being with our First Place 4 Health family.

March 2009

Vicki Heath came in for our First Place 4 Health planning meeting at Round Top Retreat. It was great seeing Euphanel and Nick Goad again and catching up from our five weeks there after Hurricane Ike.

Lisa and I drove to Austin, Texas, after our planning retreat to attend the wedding of Jim Bob and Erin, friends of my granddaughter, Cara, and her husband, Michael. Erin and Jim Bob have been to the Bay many times over the last seven years, so it was a joy being there for their wedding. Lisa and I stayed with our long-time friends Joy and Paul Stephens. Paul was the pastor of Long Point Baptist Church, where I worked for 10 years, and Joy has been one of my best friends since the early 1960s. We raised our two boys together and it is always a joy to see each other.

I went to Nashville for a business meeting and was able to see my friend Bruce Barbour while there.

I was in Dallas the end of the month for the Evangelical Christian Publishers Association meeting. The turnout was not what they expected, but I enjoyed visiting with other writers and speakers.

I am diligently working on the *Give God a Year* book again and forgot a couple of important appointments because I have been so focused on getting this book finished.

April 2009

Writing these journal pages makes me tired. I don't realize how much I do until I write it all down!

This month, I flew to San Antonio for the taping of the Paula White television show. This was a one-day turnaround trip, so I was tired that evening when I got home.

On the Thursday night before Easter, we went to our church's annual "Broken For You" service, which is always meaningful because we come together to remember our Lord's death and partake of the Lord's Supper together.

We went to two funerals Easter Week, which is always hard. One was for a Christian friend who lived to be 96 years old. The other was for a dear friend who died at 57 after battling breast cancer for 23 years.

We spent Easter with family, which is always wonderful. The week after Easter, Johnny and I made a quick trip to Los Angeles to see his oncologist.

The last week of April, I took a wild television interview tour through five states and Canada. I opted for this instead of doing one trip a week for six weeks, as that seemed like a worse plan than doing it all at once. The crazy part was that the airline lost my luggage on the second day of the trip—I had nothing but my carry-on when I landed in Toronto. Because I was in a different city every day, the luggage kept missing me; it was sent first to Toronto, then to Chicago and finally caught up with me the next-to-last night in Atlanta. A friend had strongly urged me to not check my luggage because of this possibility, but I'd said that I couldn't possibly make the trip on so few outfits. Well, I found out that I could, and I did!

May 2009

May was another busy month. I have kept my weight loss at six pounds, but I'm still struggling. I am so grateful that I haven't gained weight during this challenging year.

I did a couple of radio interviews for First Place 4 Health this month. Lisa and I traveled to Eastland, Texas, for Michael's, my grandson-in-law, college graduation on May 9. It was great being with Cara and Michael and all the family that weekend.

Johnny and I went to my fiftieth high-school reunion on May 22 and 23. It was great seeing so many old friends who share so many wonderful memories. Johnny had a great time because he graduated from Spring Branch High School two years before I did and knew many of the guys from playing football and baseball together.

June 2009

The Gospel Light team was here for a meeting on June 4, and there have been lots of meetings getting ready for our transition to a separate 501(c)3 non-profit ministry. Lots of work on a brand-new website for First Place 4 Health, along with all the legalities of separating after 28 years of being a ministry of First Baptist Church of Houston. We are very excited, but it has been a huge task all year to make it happen on July 1.

On June 26, Johnny and I celebrated our fiftieth wedding anniversary. Who would have believed that we would make 50 years after his cancer diagnosis in 1997? Thank You, God. On June 27, we flew to Honolulu with our two kids and their spouses. We boarded a Norweigan Cruise ship, *Pride of America*, for a seven-day tour of the Hawaiian islands. The kids surprised us with a limo to take us all to the airport, and what fun we had toasting sparkling grape juice during the ride! The cruise was fabulous and Johnny felt good the entire trip, making the two long plane rides just fine. The one reason Johnny and I had never wanted to go on a cruise was because of the "eating orgy" stories I had heard from so many friends who went on cruises. Sure enough, the stories were true and it saddened me to see entire families wearing size 4X T-shirts as they ate their way through the week and on to an early death.

July 2009

July was yet another busy month. We returned home from the cruise on Sunday, July 5, and I left July 10 for Denver to attend the annual Christian Bookseller's Convention. I was dreading it because I had already been away from home for a week, so I asked the Lord to give me divine appointments while I was in Denver. I had only a couple of interviews and one book signing scheduled, and I didn't want the week to be a waste of time. Well, God answered my prayers, big time! I had so many divine appointments that I had to call Pat every afternoon to unload all the information so I didn't forget anything!

I returned home on July 16, and the next Thursday our annual Leadership Summit began at our church in Houston. We had 142 attendees from 23 states, and it was a glorious time together. We had 21 of our First Place 4 Health networking leaders here on Thursday evening, and then the Leadership Summit was held all day Friday and Saturday. It was sad for all of us to not be able to go to our home at the Bay on Saturday as we have done every year.

August 2009

August brings the wrap-up of the *Give God a Year* book. The copyedits are in and I spent all day on August 7 making suggested changes and adding material. I spent a lot of time praying before I started, and I was so grateful that I got it all done in one day. It was a 12-hour day, but just one, nonetheless.

On August 13-15, we had a First Place 4 Health Change Your Life event in McKenzie, Tennessee. During the two weeks before the event, I did a couple of radio interviews by phone in the McKenzie area. I flew to Nashville on Thursday and was picked up by one of our networking leaders, Martha Norsworthy. Martha drove me to her hometown of Murray, Kentucky, where I spoke to some area pastors about the First Place 4 Health program. Friday morning, I did a radio interview and a book signing at the local bookstore in Murray before Martha drove me to McKenzie for the CYLE there on Saturday.

I am a richly blessed woman to be able to do what I love best in the entire world. The First Place 4 Health people are truly family to me and they make my job the best one around.

This is the last month of my year with God, and it is a bittersweet time for me. I have done some things really well and fallen short on others. Some of the things I have done well on "my part" are having quiet time every day, exercising every day I work, moisturizing my face and heels before I go to bed and writing in my planner for the next day's work. The areas I've struggled with are starting a strength-training program, avoiding sugary, high-fat desserts and completing everything on my list before reading or working a Sudoku puzzle.

God, of course, has done a superb job on His part, and the only reason I am not at my weight goal is because of my disobedience, choosing to feed my emotions after Hurricane Ike. God and I will get it done next year, and I will give Him all the praise and all the glory because I have proven I can't do it without Him. I am grateful for the six-pound weight loss.

God knew all that we would be going through this year, and it was sweet of Him to invite me to stay close to Him during such a trying 12 months. He has been my strength and my shield the entire year. He has done a superb job of taking care of His homeless kids. I have had very little sadness or distress because of His power to uphold during times of trial. He truly is the God of hope (see Romans 15:13) and the God of peace (see 1 Thessalonians 5:23).

I'll sign up again on August 24, 2009, for year two with God. He truly has changed my life forever this last year. I've learned so much more than I would have ever believed—things I didn't already know about Him. His love for me, His watchcare over me and His using me in spite of myself never cease to bring joy to my soul.

TESTIMONIES

Jan Norris
Topeka, Kansas

In October 2007, I arrived in Round Top, Texas, a physical wreck. I was a diabetic on insulin weighing well over 300 pounds who could barely walk without getting out of breath. I avoided stairs at all costs and had given up all hope of ever losing weight and keeping it off. I knew nothing about the First Place 4 Health program except what I had read on the Internet while searching for a Christian health spa, and from a book by Carole Lewis that I had purchased after signing up to participate. Talk about a leap of faith—I had jumped in with both feet!

Then I met Carole and my amazing First Place 4 Health family. I spent a week immersed in their love and encouragement, doing a daily Bible study called *Renewing Hope*, meeting with the Lord and drawing closer to Him. I also completed several exercise classes, and walked an incredible 59,360 steps through His strength. Before the week was over, I told Carole on an early morning walk that next year I would return and she would see a lot less of me; I was setting a goal of losing 100 pounds. Little did I imagine all the other changes that would occur in that year.

Through the years, I had lost weight many times, using just about every diet you could name, including low-carb, grapefruit, cabbage soup, diet pills and everything in between . . . but I always regained the weight and more. What I discovered through First Place 4 Health was that I had only been addressing the physical side of a four-sided person who desperately needed balance in her life. When I surrendered totally to Christ, He gave me the strength to do what I could not do alone. Losing weight is hard work, but He is faithful to provide each day what I need to "run with perseverance the race set before us" (Heb. 12:1) if "I press on toward the goal to win the prize for which God has called me heavenward in Christ Jesus" (Phil. 3:14).

Hebrews 12:1 has become my life verse, and God confirmed it to me in several ways. I arrived at Round Top with a T-shirt in my suitcase bearing that verse, only to discover that it was the week's memory verse. Then in April 2008, I entered my first 5K race. The race's theme was Hebrews 12:1! Now I have another T-shirt, a travel mug and even a backpack to remind me of those precious words. On race morning, I arrived at the starting line and immediately wanted to go home when all the "jocks" started strutting around and stretching. As I pondered doing just that, my Provider, the Lord God, brought a former student into my path. Her mom was recovering from knee problems and needed someone to walk with. Praise God for Valerie, who walked every step of the way with me (and a few extras when we got off course because everyone else was so far ahead that we couldn't see them anymore). I was encouraged and got to share my First Place 4 Health experience with her as we walked the entire route in a blazing time of 1 hour, 2 minutes and 39 seconds!

Scripture memorization was not something I had done for many years, but what a blessing it is to have words the Holy Spirit can bring to mind when I need them. For example, at Royal Family Kids Camp in June, I was thinking, "I can't do this, Lord. It's too hot and I'm too tired and too discouraged to minister to these kids." Then the Holy Spirit reminded me that "I can do everything through Him who gives me strength" (Phil. 4:13). The battle in my mind is ongoing, but I am learning to think about those things that are true, noble, right, pure, lovely, admirable, excellent or praiseworthy, as Philippians 4:8 instructs me to do. "Stinkin' thinkin'" still creeps in sometimes, but I have Scripture to combat it so that I can walk in victory.

A critical part of success in First Place 4 Health is encouragement from and accountability to others, but when I returned home to Topeka, Kansas, from Round Top, there was not a group for me to attend. I drove to Overland Park—65 miles each way—for several months. and was blessed by the leadership of Jan Rice and fellowship with a tremendous group of encouragers. After a few months, I started my own First Place 4 Health group at my home church, and that group has since become two. God has blessed me with a dozen members who encourage, uplift and hold each other and me accountable.

This fall, a woman I encouraged at RFK camp started her own First Place 4 Health ministry at her church, and my prayer is that this is only the beginning of what God will do in Kansas. So many here need the program, with obesity and diabetes on the rise, especially in our children. I spent years as a terrible role model of health and wellness in a middle school, but now my students and colleagues see the change in me. Several have joined me in wearing a pedometer and walking their way to better health. My prayer is that I can be used by the Lord to spread the good news of Christ as I spread the message of health and wellness through First Place 4 Health.

Spiritual growth has been the best part of this entire process. My daily quiet time is something I anticipate each morning. Whether it is spent outdoors walking and talking with the Lord or inside curled up on the couch with a cup of coffee or hot tea, it is a critical part of my life. First Place 4 Health Bible studies are so well written, and the Lord has used them to draw me closer to Him. Until I went to Wellness Week, I had never kept a spiritual journal, but now it is a critical part of my walk with Christ. As I look back through the pages, I can see God's faithfulness in my life as I re-read prayers and praises to Him. I am learning that feeding on His Word is better than any food I crave—and it doesn't bring guilt from overeating!

This year in October, I arrived at Round Top as another person in so many ways: an incredible 100 pounds lighter, no longer using insulin, leading two First Place 4 Health groups at my church, and acting as the First Place 4 Health networking leader for Kansas. I have walked over 1,400 miles, biked over 100 miles and taken the stairs just because I can!

What's next? I'm waiting on God to tell me, but I already know He has big plans for me in my First Place 4 Health ministry. I'll be at Wellness Week next year, and I can hardly wait to see what incredible changes the Lord will do in me when I give Him another year. I invite you all to join me at the First Place 4 Health Leadership Summit or Wellness Week at Round Top next year (see www.firstplace4health.com/events) . . . but especially I encourage you to get on the road to health and run with perseverance the race set before you!

Thank You, Father, for this incredible journey to health and wellness and for how far we have walked together. Daily be my strength and my guide as I keep my eyes on the prize for which You have called me heavenward in Christ Jesus, and may I run with perseverance the race set before me. I commit this year to You one day at a time. I love You, Daddy. Your precious princess, Jan

Patricia Bailey

Montoursville, Pennsylvania

When I was first asked to contribute my testimony to this book, I was a bit apprehensive. I haven't lost a lot of pounds or dropped several dress sizes. In fact, I've lost less than 20 pounds and only one size in a year. But First Place 4 Health is about a lot more than losing weight, and I feel my story may inspire someone.

I grew up in an abusive home and was physically, emotionally, mentally and sexually abused. I was a very angry teenager and turned to drugs, alcohol, sex and cutting for comfort. My young adult life didn't turn out much better. I was married to a man who abused me and left me when my daughter was two days old. I had no job, no family and a premature baby to care for. I was able to scrape myself up, get a job and hook a man that could pay for some of the things I needed to survive.

I felt as if God didn't care about me. Actually, I felt as if no one could ever care about me; I didn't even care about myself and wanted nothing more than to end my life. But I had this little girl who needed me, and she deserved better. So even though I hated my life, I had to stay alive to take care of her.

The years went on and I married and divorced a few more times. I never confronted the pain I had gone through as a child. Because I wanted to be a good example to my daughter, I did stop the drugs—but I substituted food in their place. There were times when the pain was unbearable. I didn't know what else to do, so I used food. In doing so, I found a great reason to hate myself even more: All the other addictions were not so visible, but the food addiction was visible and it gave me another reason to abuse myself.

I've spent so many years chasing the dream of being thin. That would make me more lovable, I thought. So I've done it all: diet fads, prepackaged foods, exercise videos, health clubs. I failed at everything, and so I thought I failed at being good enough to be loved.

In July 2005, I had been going to a personal trainer for several months. I was doing well with strength-training, but for some reason I was gaining weight. In desperation, I asked my trainer what I was doing wrong. He told me that I didn't have Jesus Christ in my life and that no matter how hard I tried, I would never be balanced until I gave my life to the Lord.

This guy was crazy! I never needed God or Jesus or anybody else. I could handle things on my own. I was proud of raising Jennifer on my own. I was proud that I had always worked, provided for and taken care of everyone around me. But I was really having a hard time taking this weight off.

Over the next few months, that trainer's words really stuck with me. Maybe I could ask God for help; what did I have to lose? I had tried everything else and wasn't ready to give up yet. I wanted to lose this weight. I went on a quest to find a church I felt comfortable with and ended up next door to my childhood home, where I continue to worship today.

A few months later, my boss told me about a Christian weight-loss program I might be interested in. I found the number, called Mary Ann and found out that it was almost time for a new session of First Place 4 Health. I hoped this would be the answer to my problems. If I could lose enough weight and be skinny, then I was sure to find a man that would love me and take care of me. My first meeting was March 26, 2007.

I approached First Place 4 Health just the same way I had approached every other "new" program I had tried. I started out of the gate sprinting, reading everything I could, making sure I did Bible study every night, memorizing the verses, filling out the Live It Tracker and even forcing myself to exercise. I was going to learn "the secret" and lose this weight quickly. But something happened that I didn't expect.

Through studying the Bible, I was learning things about myself. Things like I was loved; I was worth being treated well; I didn't have to feel guilty for the bad things I had done; and I didn't have to feel shame for the things that were done to me. I started little by little to find a peace I had never experienced before. I also found that I didn't have to be alone. The Lord was with me the whole time, and all I needed to do was to allow Him in. Old habits and feelings that had lived inside me for years started to slip away. I was able to start trusting people again. The Lord gave me the most incredible gifts and the most wonderful friends who accept me exactly the way I am.

I am still working on weight loss. Praise God, the physical recovery isn't coming to me quickly; the Lord is giving me the time I need to learn to depend on Him. If the weight had dropped off too fast, I don't know if I would have stayed with the program. I would have accomplished the weight loss and been on my way, and missed out on the greatest gift this program has given me: spiritual healing.

I am now equipped to deal with the real problems behind my overeating. I am eating healthy foods. I feel confident. I have found an exercise regimen that I not only can tolerate, but that I actually love—I am even leading the exercise portion of our First Place 4 Health group meeting. I am learning that I don't need abusive people in my life. I am learning to take care of myself on so many levels, because I really do love myself.

But I must say, the best thing I have received from this program is the changes I have made as a mother. Through finding God and myself, I have been able to relax and love Jennifer at a deeper level than I ever have before. I will never forget about six months after I started the program, Jenn and I sat outside on our front porch and talked for hours about her hopes, dreams, fears, interests and whatever else happened to come up. She told me how different I had become and how much easier it was to talk to me—and her words are something no amount of weight loss could ever give me.

I love this program, my home group and all of you, but most of all I love God for all the blessings I have received.

It has been a year since I gave this testimony at a First Place 4 Health Conference. I am awestruck at the work the Lord is accomplishing in my life. I have come to realize that deep wounds take time to heal. Right now, God is healing me from the inside out. Without First Place 4 Health, I wouldn't have had the tools to face the issues behind my eating addiction. I have been blessed with true peace and happiness, and in God's time I know the weight loss will come.

Sherry Mazza

Bayville, New Jersey

I have been married to a wonderful man for 29 years. We have three grown children—two boys and our youngest, our daughter, is in college. My two grandchildren are the light of my life. All of my children were home-schooled through high school. I have always been active in children's ministries and in leadership in our home-school association. After my daughter left for college, I felt led to minister to other women. One season in my life ended and another began.

For years, I suffered from clinical depression. Because I was depressed, I felt like a failure to God. Then I gained a lot of weight and felt even worse. I developed a lot of health problems. I didn't know that my life was not about me trying and striving to be a Christian; it was only through First Place 4 Health that I learned it is about surrender and trusting Him, seeking Him each time I have to make a choice.

After joining First Place 4 Health, I learned to have a quiet time each day to renew my mind in the Word. I really didn't begin to lose weight that first year, but the Lord was healing me on the inside. My prayer that year was for focus. Gradually, my depression began to lift and I started to lose weight. I was able to get my diabetes under control, and the four shots of insulin a day stopped. The high blood pressure and anti-depressant medication I took were no longer needed.

The Lord has renewed my mind with His truth and is showing me how much He loves me and how much grace He has for me each day. I am now able to memorize Scripture. I no longer go to church on Sunday looking to be fed on the Word of God, but am drawn by Him daily to spend time with Him. He has healed me of childhood abuse, mental illness (terrible debilitating depression) and many physical ailments.

The Lord has been with me all along my life; I just needed to learn to listen to the Holy Spirit about the goodness, grace and mercy my heavenly Father has for me. Through First Place 4 Health and the encouragement of other members, I have developed a healthy rhythm in my life, filled with the Word of God and prayer. I have begun to see in my heart how God really sees me—as blessed, redeemed, adopted, forgiven, chosen and loved. This has brought me to a better understanding of how much He cares for us.

The by-product of my renewed relationship with God is a weight loss of 80 pounds. I now weigh about 140 pounds. I once could barely walk, and now I can walk miles every day. First Place 4 Health friends have accepted and encouraged me all along the way. Because of their comfort and the healing I have received from the Lord, I am leading a group at my church and also serving as a First Place 4 Health networking leader. My life could only be changed by our God. He has given me the privilege of serving Him and comforting others with the comfort He gives me. To Him be all the glory!

Joyce Ainsworth

Brandon, Mississippi

People say a picture is worth a thousand words. I agree! A picture also reveals truth, just like the scales do. That is probably why I never really liked having my picture made. I have avoided the truth, like many of us have a tendency to do.

I hear so many people say, "I want to be small again" or "I wish I were the size I was way back when," but the truth is that I have always been big. My "family heritage" has been that we are all big. I have never known anything else. I, like so many others, have used all the excuses in the book for why being overweight is acceptable and unavoidable, lies I told myself for way too many years. I have also tried every diet and weight-loss program ever created. Sure, I would lose a small amount of weight, but then I would go back to my old lifestyle and all the weight came back, plus a little more.

A few years ago, out of sheer desperation, I started attending a First Place 4 Health class. I said to myself, "This is your last hope!" I was so miserable, discontent and unhappy with myself. The smile on my face was a fake, and it covered much pain and suffering. I kept asking the Lord to free me from this desperate battle that I seem to constantly fight within myself. How could a Christian struggle with this bondage?

I weighed in at 339 pounds. I had much to lose, so much that I almost gave up hope. However, with the help of some great leaders, a wonderful support system and much commitment and sacrifice, I made it through that first session of First Place 4 Health. And I can honestly say God has radically changed my life! Jeremiah 33:3 is my life verse: "Call to me and I will answer you and tell you great and unsearchable things you do not know." When I committed to First Place 4 Health, He began to make that verse very real to me. It is a promise from the heart of God to me that has sustained me through this journey. I am not alone! The God of the Universe loves me and wants to help me.

What a journey God has allowed me to travel! In September 2006, we started our first First Place 4 Health class at Crossgates. I weighed 226 pounds, 113 pounds lighter than the first class. In August 2007, I weighed in at 192 pounds. I started a new class in January 2008 at 184 pounds, wearing a size 14 pant. As my journey continued through September 2008, I finished that class in a size 12 and a new weight of 176 pounds!

My journey has been long and hard, but my God has been faithful! He is not done yet. Today I completed the 2009 spring session at 164 pounds and wearing a size 10. Think the journey is over? Never! God revealed to me that it is through the journey that He teaches us His ways so that we become more like Him.

I have lost 175 pounds (a whole person!), but what I have gained far outweighs what I have lost. God has given me new life, and it started on the inside. Because of the changes made there, God has changed the outside, too! The most important thing I have gained is freedom from the bondage of overeating. I am no longer enslaved to the power of food. When Christ sets us free, we are free indeed!

First Place 4 Health has given me the opportunity to become all Christ wants me to be. I have learned that balance is necessary in all parts of my life. This is not a diet, but a lifestyle change—and the truth is, my old life was never a good one and certainly not one I'd go back to!

My journey is not over, and I am thankful that the Lord is not finished with me yet! The most important thing for you to know is that I am committed to serving Jesus Christ through First Place 4 Health. I believe this program works, but it only works because of Jesus! He is the center and focus of this journey that we are embarking on together. Get ready! God is about to radically change your life. I can honestly say He has truly changed mine.

Friends, I do not consider myself yet to have taken hold of it.
But one thing I do: Forgetting what is behind and straining toward
what is ahead, I press on toward the goal to win the prize for
which God has called me heavenward in Christ Jesus.
Philippians 3:13-14

Luann Fisher
Winfield, Iowa

I grew up heavy, and food was always a source of comfort to me. I became a believer in 1993, and God began to clean up my heart one layer at a time.

The first weekend in November 2006, I attended a Christian conference as a guest of a friend. During the conference, which focused on repentance and renewing your relationship with God, the speaker spoke on sins that separate us from God. In the conference booklet, there were two pages of sins that could separate us from God. During one of the exercises, we were asked to check all of them that applied. (Ouch!) Later, as we worked our way through them one at a time, the speaker said, "Those of you who are struggling with treatment of your 'temple,' overeating is abusing the temple of God; therefore, it is sin. And you know who you are." It was a simple statement, but it penetrated my heart. I knew this was one more place that God was asking me to submit to Him.

Even in today's world, where so much focus is placed on fitness and health as well as beauty, I hadn't spent much time thinking about being overweight as sin. I had been struggling with some weight and diet-related health problems, but somehow the connection had alluded me (or maybe I had really just been in denial). My blood pressure was elevated and was barely under control with medication. My knees and hip hurt, and my feet were killing me. I was terribly out of shape; a long set of stairs was a huge challenge, and I had a constant struggle with Irritable Bowel Syndrome.

The following Sunday at church, I asked two friends to pray for me and hold me accountable. I told them I was sure that I needed to find some kind of an accountability group. One of them told me that a mutual friend was going to start a group, and the focus was to be holding us accountable for any area of struggle we might have. I called our mutual friend on a Sunday evening, and found out that the group was starting on Tuesday morning. Tuesday "happened" to be one of the days I had some flexibility in my schedule, and I could make the meeting.

One of the non-negotiables of the group was that if you were there for weight loss, you had to track your food intake in some manner. It could be any way you chose, but you had to track it. I had been reading one of Carole Lewis's books, *First Place*, at the time and was familiar with the exchange program. I had successfully lost 50 pounds about 20 years before and kept it off for 5 years by counting exchanges. Unfortunately, I stopped counting them and the pounds returned and brought more with them.

When I stepped on my home scales that Sunday morning, I weighed 298 pounds. I was tired and scared, but I knew that I had to do something to change. So, I began to do as much reading about First Place 4 Health as I could. I started with the *Healthy Holidays* Bible study, and it got me through to the first of the year. By then, our entire group had checked out the program and decided to start using the studies together. We began studying and following the program in earnest in January.

My group has been an excellent source of support for me. I still struggle with daily disciplines, but one day at a time, one victory at a time, I'm getting there. To date, I have lost 67 pounds. I still have 46 pounds to go to reach my goal. I have been stuck on a plateau since the middle of August, but I have been learning some things through it. Plateaus are just a stepping-stone on the way down. They are inevitable and unavoidable, and God is still God. He is still on the throne, even when the scale doesn't go down the way I would like.

Filling out a Live-It Tracker daily keeps me on track. I don't do it all perfectly every day, but I have come so far since last November. My relationship with the Lord is stronger; I have tons more energy; my blood pressure is down to a manageable range and my feet almost never hurt, nor do my knees and hip.

Exercise, while still a struggle for me, is slowly becoming part of my weekly routine. I'm learning to turn to a good walk and prayer time instead of Reese's Peanut Butter Cups to help me cope with life's stresses. I require less sleep and am not as moody. I haven't had an irritable bowel attack in months. I have gone from size 26W jeans to 18R.

Most of all, God has sent me a fabulous group of women who cover a range of ages and sizes. We have become extremely close. I believe that the group is one of the real keys to success. They lift me up when I need it and cheer me on at each victory. I truly love these women. My husband and son have been a great support to me also, cheering me on at every victory and holding me up through tough spots.

My "before" picture was taken on the first Sunday in November 2006. The "after" picture was taken Labor Day weekend, 2007. The "tail" I'm holding is the amount I had to have cut out of a belt I had made by a leather craftsman in September 2006. He took the picture as a trophy for me before he cut it off.

One of my great victory moments was when my family and I traveled to Six Flags. We hadn't gone in years because I knew I couldn't fit in the seats on the roller coaster. While we were waiting in line for the first roller coaster of the day, my husband, knowing how nervous I still was about fitting in the seat, leaned down and whispered in my ear, "Stop worrying! You *are* going to fit." And I did!

I'll admit that when I look in the mirror, I still see the bigger me—but she's slowly and surely shrinking. I still have a long way to go to my goal, but I believe that with God's grace and the sustaining power of the Holy Spirit, together with the love and support of my family, friends and First Place 4 Health group, I'll eventually reach my goal weight.

Don Steffey
Murray, Kentucky

At some point last fall, I reached my maximum weight ever of 424 pounds. That is a lot of weight, even at 6 feet, 3 inches. I could not walk without becoming short of breath. You would think a registered nurse would know better than to get in that kind of shape, but I'm here to tell you that it's not *what* you know, it's *Who* you know.

I believe that God brought Martha Norsworthy and the First Place 4 Health program to Grace Baptist Church to save my life. I don't think I would have lived much longer in the shape I was in. I don't know why God chose me, but oh how grateful I am.

The weight loss has been tremendous. As of last Sunday, I weighed 279 pounds, a 145-pound weight loss over just two sessions in the program. Isn't God good? I have become active in our Wellness Center, going almost every day to exercise and work out. I never would have believed this possible for me. I couldn't go there when I first started exercising last fall. I began by walking in my neighborhood. I started with short walks and gradually got the confidence to go to the Wellness Center. Now, I'm practically addicted to exercise. Thank You, God!

The weight loss and the exercise are wonderful, but they aren't everything God has done in my life. I read my Bible daily and really enjoy the Bible studies that come with the First Place 4 Health program. I can feel God working on me and in my life almost every minute I live.

I have gone through a lot of sizes in my clothes in the last six to eight months. I love for someone to comment about my weight loss, because it gives me the opportunity to say the name of Jesus, to tell about His love and give Him the glory He so richly deserves for His work in my life. Thank You, God, for this service You have given me.

The components of First Place 4 Health are not grievous. Writing down what I eat helps me know if I'm eating what I should—enough, but not too much. Drinking water is so important. I now love to drink a glass of water every chance I get.

Prayer time with God helps me start each day off right and get in a right relationship with my Maker. He loves us and wants to spend time with us. I don't know why or how He could love such as me, but I know He does. I love to be able to encourage someone to stay faithful to First Place 4 Health. Emailing is my favorite method.

I'm not perfect; I stumble and fall on this program. Occasionally, I go on a huge binge and overeat so much I hurt. But unlike other programs, God helps me to get back on course. In the past when I would binge, I just wouldn't go back on the diet. I would think, "Well, I've blown it; I might as well just give up." But First Place 4 Health is different. We believe you can have anything you want if you control the portion size.

I work nights at the local hospital. Cereal with skim milk and some type of fruit is one of my meals every day. I buy frozen fruit, divide it into portion sizes and keep it frozen in individual baggies to add to my cereal. Peaches, strawberries, blueberries and blackberries are all available in large bags in the frozen food section.

For work, I buy microwavable soup and eat it with crackers. I eat several servings of fruit daily. I often eat carrots and/or celery as snacks at work. Occasionally, I rely on Revival Soy bars for part of my protein or meat servings.

I hope this is encouraging to someone. I pray I will continue in obedience to God and stay the course. Pray for me.

Update 1

It has been a couple of years since I gave my First Place 4 Health testimony. I haven't lost another pound. Correction: I have lost and gained several pounds over the past year or two, but my weight is still around the 283 level of two years ago.

Is this a failure? Absolutely not! God has graced me with opportunities to testify to many people because of my weight loss and changes in lifestyle He has given me. Every time someone asks about the changes in me, I get to tell them about my Lord and Savior and what He is doing for and in me. Praise God for opportunities.

I go to the Wellness Center five or six times weekly and walk/run on the treadmill, or use the elliptical stepper. Every other day I lift weights. This brings me in contact with many people, and opportunities to testify are everywhere. I don't know the percentage of my body fat three years ago, but one year ago it was 22.8 percent. This is a victory!

I am the old man on our church softball team and I love to be out in the heat playing ball with the kids. I mow my own yard every week, as well as my mom's yard.

As a nurse in our local hospital, I get to talk to a lot of professionals about diet, exercise and our First Place 4 Health program. Recently, a unit secretary asked me when the program started again, and to let her know as she was going to join. Praise God, He can use even me in His work right here.

First Place 4 Health for me started three years ago when Martha Norsworthy came to our church and began teaching the program. I have participated every session since. Yes, I haven't lost any weight this year, but neither have I gained back the 140 pounds I lost the first year. Praise God and give Him glory.

I still eat cereal and microwave soup, as well as lots of fruit, and strive to get my vegetables when I have time to fix them. Water is my favorite beverage, as well as black coffee and Diet Cokes. I drink at least eight glasses of water every day.

I started re-reading my Bible three years ago. Our first memory verse was from Philippians, and I read to the end of the book, then to the end of the New Testament. I went back to Matthew and read to where I started in Philippians. Then I started in Genesis and now I'm re-reading it again. (Sounds a little like Forrest Gump). I don't read a lot each day, but I read something each day. In three years, I have been in God's Word most every day (one or two chapters), more if they are short. I love to start my day in His Word after praying for what Solomon asked for (look it up if you don't remember!). I also ask God every day to be a "lamp unto my feet and a light unto my path" (Ps. 119:105).

Reading God's Word, doing the Bible studies, encouraging others—these keep me sane and give me a reason for being. I can share my Lord Jesus without fear, without shame or doubt. Daily, God reveals more and more of His wonderful love and His plans for my life.

My lifestyle has changed, but I'm still the same. I have to guard against terrible binges of unhealthy foods. Pray for me. But for the grace of God, I would be much more than a 424-pound man by now; I would more than likely be dead.

Update 2

One hundred and sixty-three pounds lost! Read through the Bible twice. Many First Place 4 Health Bible studies completed. So much water; so much exercise. This is what God has done for me. Where I am, where I was, where I could be. God is so good! He is blessing my life daily in so many ways. I asked for help and there He was. I needed His help in my relationships, finances, health, home, family, work . . . and there He was.

He has always been here; I just didn't recognize Him completely.

I'm not there yet. God is working on me every day. I sometimes get into such a mess, but God helps me get things back in order. Walking with Him is such a blessing and adventure. I pray for ways to share Him daily and get such joy in telling what the Lord is doing in my life.

For six months I have been on what the hospital calls the Healthy Employee Program. I just completed it and want to share where God has taken me. My cholesterol is 135, triglycerides 47, fasting glucose 80. My body composition has gone from 17.8-percent body fat to 13.9 percent in 6 months. This puts me in the national ninety-second percentile, or excellent range.

But I'm still not where I want to be! I don't know what my weight should be yet, but I do want to lose two to four more inches in my waist. It will happen! I've never had the patience I needed for this until this session. I don't have to be perfect; I can't be perfect. But when I stumble or when I fall, God is right here picking me up again.

I'm praying for the peace of God for all of you. I pray for success in your life. Struggle is vital; I believe God demands we do our part. But God wants us to succeed and He is right here to help.

Larry Johnson
San Antonio, Texas

I was athletic in high school and a triathlete/marathon runner as a young adult. After hitting middle-age, I gained almost 10 pounds a year following my Army retirement. At 40, I accepted Christ, which was a life-changing experience. Over time, however, I slid away from reading the Bible daily and the accountability of my small group of more mature believers. My family and core relationships became marked with increasing bouts of anger, rebellion and a lack of desire to serve others.

I suffered mounting weight-related health issues. I could not walk up flights of steps without becoming winded. While snow skiing, I often fell down and struggled to even stand up. I was diagnosed with obstructive sleep apnea and told to wear a CPAP mask to bed. At first, I made subtle agreements with the devil that overeating was a personal little sin, yet over time that shifted to a gradual hopelessness of permanent obesity.

In January 2007, I came up with many reasons not to join Community Bible Church's initial offering of First Place 4 Health. Yet being out of control, my need was awakened and I was led to reluctantly attend the orientation in March 2007. I was anxious yet found a welcoming leader in Doug, plus real Christian male support. The commitments of the program became a foundation for a radical spiritual and lifestyle change, as

I found encouragement in this small group of big men with tender hearts for the Lord.

By my birthday in June 2007, I had lost 27 pounds by putting God first instead of my self-serving habits, plus was blessed by a band of brothers in our mega-church. Over the next year, through four First Place 4 Health Bible studies, the Lord revealed that "it's not about the weighing, but the praying." I did not have to rely on my own strength to fulfill my commitments. A First Place 4 Health memory verse, Zechariah 4:6, captures the real spiritual power in my changed heart: "Not by might nor by power, but by my Spirit, says the LORD Almighty."

At the June 2008 First Place 4 Health celebration dinner, I got an "encourager" award. That was very humbling, as this recognition meant far more to me than being the "biggest loser." Our life group just began our sixth study with First Place 4 Health, *Celebrating Victory*. I'm thankful to guide our summer study, while our founding leader takes a well-deserved break.

The bottom line is that God has used First Place 4 Health as the way to lose 75 pounds—my goal weight. The real breakthrough is that I read God's Word daily and am growing closer to my Lord. I strive to pray for the needs of the brothers in my group and they lift up mine. My health is restored, as I no longer wear a CPAP mask to bed. I strive to be a daily walker and have much more energy to serve my supportive family. I guard against judging overweight people, as without the Lord in first place in my life, I would be looking in the mirror. Please don't look to me, for if you are looking for encouragement, I would only point you to First Place 4 Health. Look to Him for all you need to keep your commitments, as our mighty God can and will exceed all expectations!

Reverend Jason A. Stevens
Waynesville, Missouri

Most of my life, I have struggled with a weight problem. I guess you could say that I was born wearing husky diapers. I always knew that I had a food addiction, but I just wasn't sure how to go about making the necessary changes in my life. I probably tried about every diet you can imagine, all to no avail. Time after time, I would once again give in to my food addictions.

Just over two years ago, I was called to serve as the pastor of a wonderful church, Church of the Nazarene in Waynesville, Missouri. The Church of the Nazarene is a holiness church. Throughout the years, we have been very outspoken against things like smoking and drinking. We've pointed to passages of Scripture like 1 Corinthians 6:19-20, which says, "Do you not know that your body is a temple of the Holy Spirit, who is in you, whom you have received from God? You are not your own; you were bought at a price. Therefore, honor God with your body." We have reminded our listeners of the sinfulness of doing damage to our physical bodies. Yet one thing has always bothered me. The question I struggled with for years as a pastor was, *If overeating does harm to my body, just like smoking or drinking, then doesn't that make it just as sinful?*

In my spirit, God convicted me that if my body is a temple of the Holy Spirit, then it's not just alcohol and cigarette addictions that are sinful—eating addictions are just as evil. So here I was, an obese preacher, calling the kettle black. There's just something wrong about a fat preacher calling a skinny smoker a sinner! According to the BMI charts, I was "morbidly obese." My food addiction was destroying God's temple and I knew it. There was no denying that I was headed to an early grave, thanks to heart disease, cancer or some other obesity-related disease.

Seven months ago, my life was changed forever. Our church's previous pastor's wife, Sharon Bushey, asked if she could start a First Place 4 Health group in our church. She mentioned that it was a Christ-centered program. I didn't understand the program completely, but I knew God had laid this on Sharon's heart. I saw the passion in her eyes for this ministry, and I gave her my blessing to move forward. Little did I know that I would be the one who would be challenged and changed the most.

As the weeks went by, and as I started embracing more and more of the First Place 4 Health program, I saw a change happening in my life. I began to see the power of God at work in my life in ways that I hadn't experienced before. I began to see God break down strongholds that were still in my life, that somehow I had managed to overlook, even as an ordained preacher of the Word. Passages of Scripture—such as "If you believe, you will receive whatever you ask for in prayer" (Matt. 21:22) and "Commit to the LORD whatever you do and your plans will succeed" (Prov. 16:3)—began to take on brand-new meaning for me.

As the pounds started coming off, my testimony grew stronger and stronger every week. And God began to give me opportunity after opportunity to share my testimony. The interesting thing is how He's used me to testify to fellow ministers of the Gospel. One such time I will never forget: I am the secretary of our local Christian ministerial alliance. Due to the holidays, it had been several months since we had last met. When we finally got together to discuss community issues, I had lost 30 or 40 pounds. As I walked into the meeting, which is held monthly at a local breakfast buffet restaurant, several of my preacher friends started commenting on how much weight I had lost and how good I looked. As one of them, who's a rather husky fellow, went to take another bite of his biscuits and gravy, he asked, "Man, how'd you do it?" I smiled and said, "I've finally learned to really put Christ first place in *every* area of my life." I guess something I said must have touched a nerve, because his smile disappeared and he put his fork down.

To date, God has helped me lose 75 pounds, but more than that, He has given me a brand-new testimony to the power of His hand at work in my life. I can now honestly say that I know this verse in 2 Corinthians 10:4 to be true: "The weapons we fight with are not the weapons of the world. On the contrary, they have divine power to demolish strongholds." Thank You, Jesus, for giving me the victory over my food addiction. Thank you to my wife, Kiley, for being my daily support system and the best helpmate a man could ever ask for. And thank you, Sharon Bushey, for your willingness to heed God's call to start this ministry and change your pastor's life forever! To God be the glory!

Kiley Stevens (Wife of Jason Stevens)
Waynesville, Missouri

Topping the scales at 211 pounds, I started the First Place 4 Health program in September 2007, with the desire only to lose weight. I was very athletic in high school and played both basketball and softball all four years. College, marriage and two kids later, I had gained 50 pounds.

I weighed 216 when I got pregnant with my first child in 2001. While I was pregnant, I was diagnosed with gestational diabetes and was put on a very strict diet, but was not required to be on insulin. A few months after my daughter was born, I became very sick. My vision became blurry and I was thirsty all the time. I went to the doctor and found out that my blood sugar was 450. They put me on a diet to see if I could control it without insulin. My blood sugar floated around 250 for a few months; I lost around 30 pounds and became very pale and sickly looking. I went to the emergency room and found out my body had gone into ketoasidosis, which is a serious condition that can lead to diabetic coma or even death.

I had lost the weight because my body was breaking down my fat for energy. I spent a few nights in ICU and was immediately put on insulin.

For the first few months, my diabetes was not controlled. I was blessed to get an insulin pump, which helps regulate my sugar by allowing my body to receive insulin throughout the day. I kept my diabetes controlled for a while after being put on the insulin pump, but went back to my old eating habits and gained back about 20 pounds.

I got pregnant with my second child in 2004, and was again put on a low-sugar diet. I thought I was eating healthy, but looking back, I wasn't. I remembered the doctors telling me that controlling my sugars in the first trimester was most important due to the risk of birth defects. I cried all night, thinking something was going to be wrong with my baby. Praise be to God, I had a very healthy boy in June 2005, and he had no signs of a diabetic mother besides being a little big.

After having my son, I tried to lose the weight again, but nothing worked. My husband and I both knew we were at unhealthy weights, but we couldn't seem to get motivated. We were then introduced to First Place 4 Health. When I first started the program, my AlC was 7.8. An A1C test measures your average blood sugar levels over a three-month period by taking a sample of hemoglobin AlC molecules, a specific component of your red blood cells. It should be under 7.0. After being in First Place 4 health for five months, I had my A1C checked again and it was 6.8. It had dropped a whole point, and I was moved from being an "uncontrolled diabetic" to a "controlled diabetic."

I'm happier, healthier and closer to Christ. He has done so much for me and blessed me beyond what I could have asked for myself. My blood sugar continues to be good and I have lost over 30 pounds so far. He is my light and my salvation and I could not have done any of it without Him. He will always be "first place" in my heart.

Heather Adams
Hanford, California

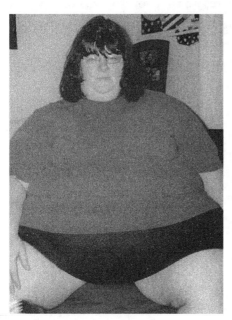 

God says that He is able to do immeasurably more than all we ask or imagine (see Eph. 3:20). I knew God, but I didn't think His promises were for me. I never took God at His word, until He made His Word a reality in my life. I had let Satan's lies hold me captive for too many years. I was so ashamed of my weight and how I looked that I hid away from the world, spending 10 years of my life in my bedroom. I wasn't living; just existing.

By July 2005, my weight had reached 435 pounds. I knew my life was slipping away from me, but I felt hopeless and helpless to change. Then God gave me the opportunity to join First Place 4 Health. I know without a doubt that my life will never be the same again. I have started on a journey with God to reclaim my life. God has used and is using the First Place 4 Health program to teach me to live as the new creation He has called me to be.

Nearly two years into my journey, I have lost 235 pounds. I am still in shock at times about how all the weight has come off. Obviously, the weight loss has been great, but I have gained so much more besides. I am a different person today than I was two years ago. I am not just physically different; I have changed spiritually, mentally and emotionally as well.

I have met some great friends over the past two years. Their support and encouragement means everything to me. Most importantly, my relationship with God has strengthened and grown me. I know God never wanted me to be overweight, but I also know God loved me at 435 pounds, just as He loves me today. I know I am unique and precious in God's eyes.

I am about 44 to 54 pounds away from my goal weight. I don't know when I will reach my goal, but I know that as long as I remain in God's love and will, He will give me the power and strength to reach my goal.

Michael Heath
Charleston, South Carolina

As I stepped off the plane, I had no idea what to expect. That was most easily evident by the warm leather jacket I quickly shed as I stepped in to the bright, sunny, 85-degree Hawaiian weather. I had come to the Big Island of Hawaii to give God a year. Well, to be honest, I had only intended to give Him three months there and then get back to the East Coast in hopes of marrying the young lady with whom I had recently been reconciled. But that's a story for another time.

At the beginning of the previous summer, I received a call from a man I had never met, but who was a long-time friend of my father's since their days at New Orleans Seminary. The reason he had called was that he had recently taken a new job as pastor of a church on the Big Island of Hawaii, and he really needed a youth pastor. God had put me heavy on his heart, so he was calling to see if I was interested in coming to Hawaii and living with him and his family to serve as youth pastor for a few months. He said he didn't have any salary, but he would get someone to loan me a car and would pay for my gas, let me live in his house and eat his food.

It took me about three seconds to decide it was a great idea, but in order to seem more wise and godly than I was, I told him I needed some time to think about it. There was one problem: I still had two semesters of college left and had already taken one semester off. I decided I would never do that again because it was so hard to go back and finish. So I began looking for ways to speed up my education and everyone at the school told me it was impossible. The classes I needed weren't offered until the next year; my grades weren't high enough for them to allow me to take more than 18 hours in a semester; I could never get permission to do it, and even if I could, the classes weren't offered. So after eight months, 30 hours, countless visits to dean's offices, begging, pleading, reading extra books, meeting with teachers one-on-one for classes that weren't offered until the next year, I walked across the stage to get my diploma, and headed for Hawaii.

I had no idea what God had in store for my life in the coming days. I had grown up in the buckle of the Bible belt, the son of preacher man. I knew all the words, sang all the songs, and even occasionally helped lead worship on Sundays. I taught Sunday School classes and Bible studies in school and led devotions before every football, basketball and soccer game I played in through high school. I was called to the ministry at the young age of 14 and knew that was where I was headed, yet nothing I had ever experienced would prepare me for my time in Hawaii. Nothing could prepare me for meeting Jesus—the real life, life-giving, soul-cleansing, spring of never-ending water, Jesus Christ. You may be wondering how I could possibly have missed Him amid all of the religious activities, and quite honestly, I don't know how—but I do know how I found Him, and that is what comes next.

The first two weeks in Hawaii turned out to be the toughest. A week into my being there, I received a call from my lady friend, whom I was so sure I was going to marry, letting me know that things weren't working out so well anymore and it was over. I was stunned, to say the least.

This forced me to realize just how dependent I had become on so many things other than God. I began to realize then that all my life I had never really depended on God for much of anything. To be honest, I had never really needed Him. Growing up, it was the church where I first found all I needed. We Southern Baptists have so many programs and activities for kids that I wouldn't dare try to list them here. When I got to high school, church became less important and the "Friday night lights" took its place—I was consumed by sports and the attention that came with it. I still never missed a moment the church doors were open; it just didn't give me what I needed anymore. The roar of the crowd was what I longed for.

Then, off to college after being the big fish in the little pond, the athlete of the year, Mr. Everything, I was immediately nobody, thrust into a world of college football I wasn't ready for—the pace, the competition, the attention, not to mention having to show up to class occasionally. I got caught in the party of life, the leader of those who tried as hard as they could to act like they didn't care about anything. I successfully filled the void with my closest friends and with the girl, so beautiful, so sweet, the cute Tennessee accent. I poured everything I had into those relationships and gave them my all. The girl would eventually become more like a god, more like a thing to be worshiped.

I had never lacked some good thing to fill me up long enough to realize the great need I had for God. So here I was more than 5,000 miles from all my fillers and, as my dad would say, I was lost as a ball in high weeds.

I was literally sick: didn't eat much for a few days, had a knot in my stomach the size of a baseball. Then Satan began to attack, and for some days I didn't sleep. Then when I slept, the dreams were nightmares like I had never had before. I would wake up in the night, not wanting to go back to sleep. I remember one day thinking, *Okay, I'm going home, going back to what I know, going back to the relationships, to the fillers, going back to get what I need. I'll get the girl back; I'll move near my buddy in Tennessee, be with my family, everything will be better then.*

Then one morning about two and a half weeks into my stay, I walked out of my room after yet another nightmare-filled night, and I saw something familiar. I was living with the pastor's family and as I walked into the kitchen, I looked into the next room and saw my pastor's wife sitting in her chair, Bible open in her lap, glasses on, spending time in the Scripture. I looked over to the kitchen table, and there was my pastor, Bible open, journal open, resource books open, spending time in the Scriptures—and then I realized what was so familiar about the moment. Every morning of my life, I had woken up to the same scene: my father in his chair in the living room, Bible open to search the Scriptures, and my mother in her room in her chair, Bible open to search the Scriptures.

I realized at that moment what my parents had that I was missing, what my new pastor here in Hawaii had, what my grandparents had: a real-life relationship with Jesus Christ. They had a relationship with Him from whom they got everything they needed. They had a relationship that was so vital for their lives that no matter what the current situation, no matter how much seminary training they had, no matter how many devotionals they had studied, the first thing they did every morning was search the Scriptures and spend time with Jesus.

And it was at that moment I had a real crisis of belief. I could either keep getting all I needed from the millions of fillers I had found so tasty all my life, or I could take Jesus at His word. I could come and take His yoke upon me, I could come and follow Him, I could decide to get all I needed straight from the hand of the greatest Giver in the history of the world . . . or I could pack it up and go home. I had a pretty serious talk with God that day, and one of the things He impressed on my heart was that I not only needed to learn His promises and figure out how to stand on them, but I also had to say no to other people and places that could serve as fillers for my heart.

So that day I began searching the Scriptures—memorizing promise after promise that God gave us through His Word, promise after promise that the Scriptures assure us will come to pass if we believe—and I said no to everything else. I said no to calling and chasing after the relationships that were so far away and so long gone. I said no to activities that would fill up my time yet still leave me empty inside. I spoke frankly with the Father each day, speaking out loud His promises for my life and demanding that He uphold His end of the bargain. I told Him I couldn't survive if He wasn't who He said He was and didn't do what He said He would do.

I read 1 John 4:4 and learned that the One in me was greater than the one in the world, and I believed it and prayed the words before I slept. And the terrible dreams ceased. I read Mathew 4:7, which says that man doesn't live on bread alone, and John 4:32: "I have food to eat you don't know about." I wanted to believe it, so I fasted for 14 days, and He fed me, nourishing my body with His Word. When I began to really believe what He said, really stand on His promises, I met Him: the Giver of Life, the One who makes all things new. I began to get everything I needed for life and righteousness from Him, and it was like the sweetest, freshest milk and honey I had ever tasted. I realized all my life I had been missing one thing: life. Jesus said, "I am life." And He really meant it. He is full life, full and overflowing.

The rest of the year was full of God working in me and through me in ways I never could have imagined. I was blessed to be a part of seeing more people come into the kingdom of God in one year than I had ever talked to about Jesus in my life. That year, God gave me the privilege of working with a pastor whose lifeblood was evangelism. He wrote Scripture verses on His golf balls and use them as a witness when he played. We went to Mardi Gras and held up signs that said "Body piercing saved my life" and used them to engage the partygoers in conversation about a Savior who loved them enough to be pierced for their iniquities.

During my year on the island, God led us to start two youth groups in two different cities. One was made up of the "in crowd"—the rich kids whose parents owned construction companies and real estate. The other was the "down and outs"—mostly local Hawaiians. Both groups had issues: drugs, PPP (pretty poor parenting), loneliness, abuse. The students and their issues were as different as night and day, but the solution to the problem was the same: Jesus. They needed the same Savior I did, and not just a walk down an aisle, not just repeating a prayer and getting baptized. These kids desperately needed what I had for so long glanced right over; they needed a real-life Jesus who loved them. They—better yet, *we*—desperately needed our lives to intersect with the living God. They needed healing from abuses of the worst kinds, rescue from drug addiction and comfort from homes that neither cared for nor wanted them. We all needed the same thing, and I believe that almost all of us found it together.

One of the most memorable ways I experienced Him that year happened one Sunday morning, about eight months into my year. I was sitting on my bed, reading my Bible a little before we headed off to church (something I never would have thought of doing before this year, mind you). The next thing I knew, the headboard started slamming against the wall and I was thrown out of the bed, my ears deafened by the roar of the earth shaking. It was an earthquake! I couldn't believe it. Never in my life have I ever experienced such awesome, raw power. In the days following the quake, the Lord led me to passages such as Psalm 104:32, "He who looks at the earth and it trembles," and Amos 9:5, "The sovereign LORD Almighty touches the earth and it quakes." Not only did we experience His power and might in our personal lives, but we experienced His greatness in nature as well.

Recently, I got an email from one of the students I was privileged to know in Hawaii. She told me how her life had become a mess all over again. The email took me back to an evening in Hawaii when this student showed up on our doorstep emotionally broken, betrayed by a close friend, having just experienced something that shook her—no doubt as much as the earthquake had that Sunday morning. I went and got my pastor's wife and we prayed and hurt with her. We searched the Scripture for God's promises of healing, forgiveness and love. Over the next few months, this young lady chose to believe the promises that God had given her. She chose to believe in the power of God in her life, and as a result, she had a real-life, life-changing experience with Jesus her Savior and the powerful God of the universe.

As I read her most recent email, she talked of poor decisions made, loneliness inside, a feeling of emptiness. As I got to the end of the email, already thinking about what advice I could give her, what direction I could point her in, I realized she didn't need my answer. At the end of the email was a simple request: "I just need to know which version of the Bible we used to read in Hawaii. There are so many kinds, and I just need to get back in the Scriptures and get my relationship with Jesus back on track." My heart was overjoyed. She really got it! She really got the message that the thing we need more than anything in life is Jesus—a real-life relationship with the living God. I immediately went online, purchased a Bible and had it sent to her house.

The stories about how I and a bunch of hoodlums from Hawaii met the true and living God in a year spent in Hawaii are endless, each one with its own twist, each student with their own need, their own emptiness, their own battle. Each student with his or her needs met, life filled to overflowing, victory found in Jesus. I'll be honest: Some of the stories didn't end so well. Some of them chose to fill themselves with things other than the spring of living water that never runs dry. But the ones who chose Jesus, the ones who had a real-life encounter with the true and living God, including myself, would never be the same. Thank God! We will never be the same.

Had I not taken that year to separate myself from all of the stuff in my life, all of the relationships and activities that had filled the God-space in my life, I'm not sure where I would be. I know that God is sovereign and always accomplishes His purposes, so I am sure I would have met Him somewhere along the line. But I am so glad, so thankful, so changed because *I gave God a year.*

Cara Symank Parker

Eastland, Texas

When Mimi [Carole Lewis] talked to me last August about her new book, *Give God a Year*, I was intrigued and asked her to pray for me this year as she wrote the book. This has been quite the year for me, my husband, Michael, and our little boy, Luke. We moved to Eastland last summer so that Michael could finish his college degree. I took a teaching job in a small district about 10 miles from our home, and a lady who has kept children in Eastland for years cared for Luke.

I must admit I was more than a little worried—I struggle with worry—about the new job and our new town. Would Luke be happy? Would I like my job? Would Michael be able to finish by May? I asked Mimi to pray for all of these worries, along with my worry problem.

We began our year in August and Luke immediately bonded with the lady who cared for him. He never cried one day when I dropped him off. This was a huge answer to prayer.

My school situation, on the other hand, was a different story. The school is a Title I school, and many of the kids are extremely poor and come from homes with a lot of dysfunction. In spite of the difficulties I have faced, I've been so grateful that God has used me in that school this past year.

One of the boys, Kyle, who is hearing impaired, started out so withdrawn and angry. He has done really well and graduated in May. His teachers talked about how he has made the biggest turnaround of any student that they have taught. They said that last year was very scary when it came to dealing with him; that they are just amazed by the fact he has done his work this year and was talking and laughing—a completely different person. I know that prayer was the reason he did so well.

I was given the opportunity to talk to a senior boy about his current situation with his girlfriend and his eight-month-old baby girl. He wanted to leave because he thought that staying was just too hard. I was given the opportunity to talk to him a little bit each day for a few weeks, and finally recommended the movie *Fireproof*. About a month later, his girlfriend began bringing their baby to school and walking with me. They are doing great. They have decided that they are going to work through the tough times so that they can raise their daughter together.

I began walking with a group of pregnant girls. Not only was I getting to walk, but it also gave me an opportunity to be able to talk to the girls. I never talked with them about religion, but I feel that they know that there is something different about me. One girl, Krystal, already had her baby and I went to the hospital when the baby was born. Two days after he was born, she called to ask my opinion on what to name him.

I believe God worked through me in my school this year, and that made it worth everything to me. Two of the best things that happened are that my husband, Michael, graduated from college in May and we are expecting a little girl, Kate Taylor, in October.

God has been so very good to us this year and we are so glad He is in Eastland, Texas, because He lives inside of us.

First Place 4 Health Leader
(Name Withheld)

"He reached down from on high and took hold of me; he drew me out of deep waters . . . He brought me out into a spacious place; he rescued me because He delighted in me" (Ps. 18:16,19). "For the Mighty One has done great things for me—holy is his name" (Luke 1:49).

Over the last three years, these verses have become the anthem of my life. We serve a miraculous God! He is in the business of resurrecting dead things and creating new, beautiful life. How do I know? He did it for me!

My husband and I were married in 1992. We were both Christians, but Christ was not the cornerstone of our marriage. As years passed, the pressures of life took a toll on our relationship. We were both desperately unhappy and looked to things of the world to numb the pain.

In 2001, the Lord grabbed hold of me and started bringing balance to the chaos of my life. I began studying His Word and spending time with Him every day. He became my lifeline and I began to change. He showed me how to become a loving mother. He saw me through the death of my father. He gave me courage to wake up in the morning and kept me through the watches of the night—yet all the while, my marriage remained in shambles.

As a "get things done" girl, I kept picking up balls I felt my husband was dropping. I determined not to be dependent on him for anything. I kept telling the Lord the long list of things that I felt needed to be changed, and I couldn't understand why the Lord was taking so long. I really was trying to live for Christ; however, I didn't recognize the plank in my own eye.

By 2006, our marriage was a choice of the will and even that faltered. Trust was broken. Counseling had failed and we even tried living apart for a short time. Our children were suffering and I resigned myself to the thought that this was my cross to bear . . . but I was about to come face to face with the depth of my sin and the awesomeness of God.

As I listened to the speaker at the First Place 4 Health Wellness Week, he started to talk about the romance between Adam and Eve. What did that have to do with wellness? Everything. The Lord showed me that I had been patting myself on the back for staying in my marriage when the truth was that I had checked out emotionally years ago. In God's eyes, there was no difference. I was broken.

The Lord sent a prophet who prayed for me and began telling me things I needed to do. How could she know? She'd never been to my home. Yet the Lord was revealing to her the secret things. I had to get off the throne in my home. She led me to 1 Peter 2:18–3:9 in the *Amplified Bible*. Through tears I copied it down, and with the help of this godly woman, I committed to doing what it said. I was scared and overwhelmed, but the Lord is gracious. Now that He had my attention, He began to teach me.

I learned that I had a tendency to try to train my husband, instead of demonstrating my love in service to him. I was trying to do the Holy Spirit's job of convicting him, instead of being his biggest cheerleader and supporter. Proverbs 16:24 says, "Pleasant words are like a honeycomb, sweetness to the soul and health to the bones" (*NKJV*). It's hard to describe the immediate benefits I saw when I began to align my actions toward my husband with God's Word.

I was also amazed to discover that I had been keeping a long list of my husband's mistakes. First Corinthians 13:5 says that love "keeps no record of wrongs." I began to pray that the Lord would enable me to love according to His prescription, forgiving as I want to be forgiven. I needed to die to self and live by His Spirit. To put this into action, I started a "record of rights." I took note when my husband did something great. I wrote in my journal about the things that first attracted me to him, to remind myself of his good qualities.

Next, I began to follow God's command not to be afraid. Nehemiah 4:14 says, "Remember the Lord, great and awesome, and fight for your brethren, your sons, your daughters, your wives, and your houses" (*NKJV*). All we have to do is "remember the Lord"—and this means getting on our knees. I began to fight for my marriage in prayer, refusing to let the enemy discourage me. I wouldn't give up, because I knew that there is no more powerful position than kneeling before the Lord in prayer.

I began to forgive my husband's past offenses and pray blessings over him. It was hard to do this at first without telling the Lord exactly how I wanted Him to fix my spouse, but with practice, I got the hang of it. I began to pursue God's description of a godly wife, in those verses from 1 Peter. That passage became ingrained in my mind as I prayed them for many months, and the Spirit helped me start living them out.

These verses go against the grain of what the world tells us. Being submissive to anyone is very difficult, and the world says that it's not worth it—or that it's dangerous! If I know my husband is making a bad decision, I shouldn't go along with it, right? Wrong. God's Word says that the Lord will guard my family as I submit to my husband, because He is the Lord of lords.

I am learning that I am not responsible for my husband's decision, but I *am* responsible for my response to him. If what he asks is not immoral or illegal, I'm learning not to argue my side but instead to say (without patronizing), "Whatever you think is best." After all, "submission" only happens when we disagree—when we agree, it's called "agreement"! Submission—God's way—is not the end of ourselves but the key to great freedom! It is richly rewarded by God. First Peter 3:1 says, "Even if any (husbands) do not obey the Word [of God], they may be won over not by discussion, but by the [godly] lives of their wives" (*AMP*).

God's Word is sharper than any double-edged sword (see Heb. 4:12). When we come into agreement with what He says and repent, He accomplishes His purposes within us (see Isa. 55:11). Our lives will be transformed by the renewing of our minds (see Rom. 12:2), as we conform not to this world, but to God's plan for marriage.

Why am I so passionate about this? Because I am living a miracle! I had given up, but God hadn't! I thought that fighting and dissension were what I could expect the rest of my life. Just when I thought that I couldn't stay for another day, God asked, *Can you stay for today?*

Now, just three years later, my husband has a new wife—and it's me! And God gave me a wonderful husband! He's my friend and I love him dearly. God is making a mighty man of God right before my very eyes!

APPENDIX C

GIVE GOD A YEAR
JOURNAL

These journal pages are for you to fill out as you give God the next year of your life. When you complete your year with God, you'll be able to see how He has walked every step with you.

GIVE GOD
A YEAR,
CHANGE
YOUR LIFE
FOREVER!

Month 1

Year

GIVE GOD A YEAR, CHANGE YOUR LIFE FOREVER!

Month 2

Year

GIVE GOD
A YEAR,
CHANGE
YOUR LIFE
FOREVER!

Month 3

Year

GIVE GOD A YEAR, CHANGE YOUR LIFE FOREVER!

Month 4

_____

Year

GIVE GOD
A YEAR,
CHANGE
YOUR LIFE
FOREVER!

Month 5

Year

GIVE GOD A YEAR, CHANGE YOUR LIFE FOREVER!

Month 6

Year

GIVE GOD A YEAR, CHANGE YOUR LIFE FOREVER!

Month 7

Year

GIVE GOD A YEAR, CHANGE YOUR LIFE FOREVER!

Month 8

Year

PRAY
OBEY

GIVE GOD A YEAR, CHANGE YOUR LIFE FOREVER!

Month 9

Year

GIVE GOD A YEAR, CHANGE YOUR LIFE FOREVER!

Month 10

Year

PRAY
OBEY

GIVE GOD A YEAR, CHANGE YOUR LIFE FOREVER!

Month 11

Year

GIVE GOD A YEAR, CHANGE YOUR LIFE FOREVER!

Month 12

Year

What Can God Do in Your Life in a Year?

Give God a Year Kit

The *Give God a Year* Kit contains everything you need to set aside one year and watch God's power change you from the inside out. Change will happen over the course of 12 months, but the right changes only happen when you set goals and take the right steps to achieve them. You will dream big about the changes you have longed for your whole life and receive practical, biblical, step-by-step guidance for seeing those dreams made into reality. In a culture of "right now," a year may seem like an eternity. A year in the hands of God, however, means change that will last eternally. The kit includes the *Give God a Year* trade book, *Give God a Year* journal, *Give God a Year* 365-day tear-off calendar, *Give God a Year* refrigerator magnet, *Give God a Year* mug, and an audio CD with a special message from national First Place 4 Health director, Carole Lewis.

Give God a Year Kit
978.08307.52133 • $49.99
available at www.gospellight.com
and www.firstplace4health.com

Experience a First Place 4 Health Miracle

Teaching New Members Is Easy!

The First Place 4 Health Kit contains everything members need to live healthy, lose weight, make friends, and experience spiritual growth. With each resource, members will make positive changes in their thoughts and emotions, while transforming the way they fuel and recharge their bodies and relate to God.

97808307.45890
$99.99 (A $145 Value!)

Member's Kit Contains:
- First Place 4 Health Hardcover Book
- Emotions & Eating DVD
- First Place 4 Health Member's Guide
- First Place 4 Health Prayer Journal
- Simple Ideas for Healthy Living
- First Place 4 Health Tote Bag
- Food on the Go Pocket Guide
- Why Should a Christian Be Physically Fit? DVD

I lost 74 pounds in 9 months!

Abby Meloy, New Life Christian Fellowship Lake City, Florida

I am thankful for the First Place program. As a pastor's wife who remained at the 200-pound (+) mark for seven years, I can now say I am 135 pounds, a size 8, and I have maintained this weight.

In the beginning, I did not want to try First Place 4 Health. I did not want to weigh my food or take the time to learn the measurements, but the ladies in my church wanted the program, and I was a size 18/20, so I gave it a shot. After our first session, I was 27 pounds lighter and had new insights that my body is the temple of the Holy Spirit. It took me 9 months and 3 sessions to lose 74 pounds.

My new lifestyle has influenced my husband to lose 20 pounds and my 13-year-old daughter to lose 35 pounds. We are able to carry out the work of the ministry with much less fatigue. I now teach others in my church the First Place program and will be forever grateful that the Lord brought it into my life.

Influence Others to Put Christ First

Starting a Group Is Easy!

The First Place 4 Health Group Starter Kit includes everything you need to start and confidently lead your group into healthy living, weight loss, friendships, and spiritual growth. You will find lesson plans, training DVDs, a user-friendly food plan and other easy-to-use tools to help you lead members to a new way of thinking about health and Christ through a renewed mind, emotions, body and spirit.

Group Starter Kit Contains:
- A Complete Member's Kit with Member Navigation Sheet
- First Place 4 Health Leader's Guide
- Begin with Christ Bible Study
- First Place 4 Health Orientation and Food Plan DVD
- How to Lead with Excellence DVD
- 25 Brochures on the First Place 4 Health Program

  978.08307.45906
  $199.99 (A $256 value!)

discover a new way to healthy living

I lost 80 pounds!

Jim Clayton, D.Min.
Senior Pastor, Dixie Lee Baptist Church
Lenoir City, Tennessee

As a pastor, the changes in my life as a result of First Place 4 Health have provided me the opportunity to more adequately equip our church family to see themselves individually as God's temple. I know of no other health program available with the biblical and doctrinal integrity provided by First Place 4 Health. I lost 80 pounds in 1993 after joining First Place 4 Health and have kept it off for the last sixteen years.

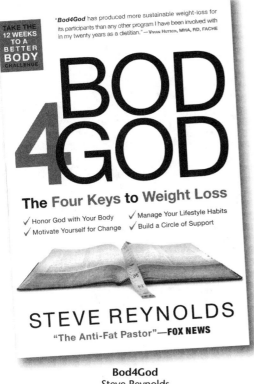